Each recipe includes the following information:

– the **number of persons** the recipe is designed for
– the **preparation and cooking time**
– the **nutritional content** per portion

The following signs and abbreviations are used:

■	= very easy
■ ■	= more demanding (complicated)
■ ■ ■	= highly demanding

kcal	= kilocalories (1 kcal=4.184 kJ)
P	= protein
F	= fat
C	= carbohydrate

NB.	1 gram of protein contains about 4 kcal
	1 gram of fat contains about 9 kcal
	1 gram of carbohydrate contains about 4 kcal

tbsp	= tablespoon
tsp	= teaspoon
pinch	= about ⅛ teaspoon

– If you are using a fan-assisted oven, the oven temperatures should be set 50°F lower than those given conventionally.

– Times and power information for microwave ovens are given individually in all microwave recipes.

INSPIRED
BAKING

AUTHORS AND PHOTOGRAPHY

BASIC INGREDIENTS AND METHODS

– Friedrich W. Ehlert –
– Odette Teubner, Kerstin Mosny –

HEARTY HOME COOKING

– Rotraud Degner –
– Pete Eising –

CAKES FROM AROUND THE WORLD

– Rotraud Degner –
– Ulrich Kerth –

RECIPES FOR SPECIAL OCCASIONS

– Marianne Kaltenbach –
– Rolf Feuz –

WHOLEFOOD RECIPES

– Doris Katharina Hessler –
– Ansgar Pudenz –

QUICK AND EASY RECIPES

– Cornelia Adam –
– Michael Brauner –

MICROWAVE RECIPES

– Monika Kellermann –
– Odette Teubner, Kerstin Mosny –

LEAN CUISINE

– Monika Kellermann –
– Anschlag & Goldmann –

Translated by UPS Translations, London
Edited by Josephine Bacon

CLB 4212
Published originally under the title "Das Neue Menu: Kuchen, Torten, Kleingebäck"
by Mosaik Verlag GmbH, Munich
© Mosaik Verlag, Munich
English translation copyright © 1995 by CLB Publishing,
   Godalming, Surrey, UK
Project co-ordinator: Peter Schmoeckel
Editors: Ulla Jacobs, Cornelia Klaeger, Heidrun Schaaf, Dr Renate Zeltner
Layout: Peter Pleischl, Paul Wollweber

Published in the USA 1995 by JG Press
Distributed by World Publications, Inc.
Printed and bound in Singapore
ISBN 1-57215-071-8

The JG Press imprint is a trademark of JG Press, Inc.
455 Somerset Avenue
North Dighton, MA 02764

INSPIRED
BAKING

JG PRESS

Contents

Basic Ingredients and Methods

*B*aking is fun, whether you are making cakes, pastry, or cookies, and there is endless scope for imaginative new recipes.

The mixture is basically the same for all these recipes: flour, eggs, and sugar, only the method varies.

The correct quantities of the individual ingredients, the preparation technique, and the choice of raising agent determine the character of the dough for cakes, sponges, sweet shortcrust, yeast dough, and many other kinds of cake. All sorts of cakes and pastries can be produced from a basic dough, by adding various flavorings, spices, nuts, and fruit.

Cakes can be topped with fresh berries or other fruit, or filled and decorated with whipped cream or frosting.

FLOUR

Milled grain is the basic ingredient of nearly every dough. You can make your own whole-wheat flour by grinding grain in a home mill, or you can buy flour of various types. The lower the extraction rate, the less the proportion of nutrients. Flour with a high extraction rate is darker and richer in protein, vitamins, minerals, and fiber than white flour. However, white flour possesses better baking qualities and is therefore preferred for cakes and pastries. The main wheat flours on the market are all-purpose flour (for general use; always use the unbleached variety); cake flour (high-gluten, highly refined, for cakes, shortcrust pastry, and cookies) and self-rising flour which is flour pre-mixed with baking powder. Brown flours are whole-wheat flour and graham flour. Graham flour is lighter than whole-wheat flour for cake baking, but is often hard to find; it has an 80% extraction rate, and is thus higher in gluten. Wholefood baking uses whole-wheat and graham flour exclusively.

CORNSTARCH

In addition to flour, cornstarch is also used in baking, for example in sponges, creamed cake mixture, and meringues. It is often substituted for some of the flour when a particularly light, fine dough is required, as its starch content inhibits the gluten. The higher the proportion of cornstarch in a sponge mixture, the lighter and fluffier the end product will be.

EGGS

Eggs contain all the nutrients we need to support life: high-grade protein, minerals, vitamins, fat, and lecithin. For baking, their raising effect makes them almost indispensable. Eggs not bought directly from a farm or a market must display the following particulars:
• Size by weight
• Packing date
• Total number of eggs
• Name and address of the producer or packer.
The USDA egg classification is by weight in ounces for one dozen eggs, as follows:-
Jumbo   30 ounces
Extra large   27 ounces
Large   24 ounces
Medium   21 ounces
Small   18 ounces
Peewee   15 ounces
In addition they are divided according to quality:
Class A and AA are fresh eggs.
Classes B and C are only used in the catering industry.

Freshness test

A fresh egg is always recognizable by the size of its air pocket: small means fresh, larger means older.

It is easy to test whether eggs are really fresh:
• Fresh eggs sink to the bottom of a glass of water.
• An egg 7 days old also sinks, but with the rounded end upward.
• Eggs more than 2 weeks old float.

MILK AND MILK PRODUCTS

Many doughs only achieve the desired consistency by the addition of milk or milk products.

Raw milk

Unpasteurized milk is neither heated nor treated in any way and has a fat content of 3.5-4%. It is not sold in many states.

Whole (full-cream) milk

This milk contains at least 3.5% fat and is pasteurized (heated before bottling) and sometimes homogenized too.

Semi-skimmed milk

Semi-skimmed milk is pasteurized and contains between 1.5% and 1.8% fat and so is lower in calories, cholesterol, and fat-soluble vitamins than wholemilk.

Nonfat (Skim) milk

Skimmed milk is pasteurized and contains less than 1% fat. It is often sold as powder.

Buttermilk

Buttermilk was once a by-product of buttermaking but today it is a cultured product made from skim milk to which lactobacillus is added.

Yogurt

Special milk-souring bacteria are responsible for the acidic flavor. Yogurt is classified by fat content, as follows: Greek-style yogurt (at least 10% fat), full-cream milk yogurt (3.5%), low-fat yogurt (1.5-1.8%), skimmed milk yogurt (0.3%). All types can be refrigerated for 2–3 weeks, except the Greek-style yogurt which may be stored for only 1–2 weeks.

Kefir

By the addition of kefir yeast part of the milk sugar is converted into alcohol, the rest into lactic acid. Kefir was originally produced from mare's milk.

Quark

The addition of rennet and lactic acid bacteria produces a soft cheese called quark which is virtually fat free. It is popular in Europe and is gradually appearing here in the better supermarkets. It is excellent for baking.

Cottage cheese and cream cheese

Both these unmatured cheeses are used in baking. Always use small-curd cottage cheese for cakes.

Cream

This is one of the richest, most versatile and useful milk products. Whipping cream contains 35% fat and heavy cream contains 48% fat. When whipped, cream should at least double in volume. The higher the fat content, the easier it is to whip.

Sour cream

The fat content of this product varies between 10% and 28%. It is suitable for cooking and baking and can be stored in the refrigerator for about 8-10 days.

Crème fraîche

This is light sour cream with at least 30% fat content and a fine acidic flavour, which can be kept in the refrigerator for about 14 days. It is not always available in the stores, but can be made at home by adding 2 tbsps buttermilk to 1 cup heavy cream and leaving first in a warm place for 24 hours, then in the refrigerator for 3 days.

SHORTENING FOR BAKING

Various types of shortenings can be used for baking. They differ in composition, consistency, and reaction to heat.

Butter

To make butter, cream is churned until it coagulates and separates out from the milk. Butter must contain exactly 82% fat and 16% water. Other ingredients make up the remaining 2%. Butter improves the flavor of baked goods. Always use unsalted butter in baking.

Clarified butter

Clarified butter or butterfat is obtained by melting and then centrifuging butter. If used in baking, the fat quantity given in the recipe can be reduced by one fifth. This fat is easy to work with because of its softer texture and because it does not burn easily.

Margarine

This valuable butter-substitute is usually easier to work than butter when baking. Margarine, also called oleo, is a pure vegetable fat, produced from plant oils and skim milk or water. Emulsifiers are added to cause the oil and water to combine into an emulsion. Vitamins, starch, and carotene are added. The oils mainly used are from the seeds of sunflower, safflower, cotton, rape, grape, peanuts, corn, and soybeans.

Butter

Butterfat

Margarine

Vegetable shortening

Vegetable shortening

Frying always demands a heat-stable fat that can be heated to as high as 355°F for long periods. Firm white hydro-genated vegetable fat is ideal. After prolonged and repeated use, shortening becomes rancid and should be thrown away. If refrigerated, it will last for months.

RAISING AGENTS

Only a dough containing several eggs, a fair amount of fat and sugar, and a little flour will rise without the help of a raising agent. All other mixtures need a raising agent to make them light and fluffy.

Yeast

This consists of living micro-organisms, yeast cells, which divide and multiply with warmth, sugar, air, and moisture. Adding some flour, sugar, and milk or water to the yeast and leaving it to stand in a temperature of 75–85°F provides it with optimum growth requirements. As the yeast grows, carbon dioxide is released, both before and during baking, which makes the dough light and well-risen.

Baking Powder

This consists of baking soda (sodium bicarbonate), acid (cream of tartar, tartaric, or citric acid) and mineral salts. Together with air, moisture and warmth, baking powder releases carbon dioxide, which lightens the baking. It is suitable for all sorts of dough, particularly those which cannot be raised with yeast. Always keep it dry so that it doesn't lose its effectiveness.

JELLING AGENTS

It is most important that light fillings are given a good cutting consistency by the addition of gelling agents.

Gelatin

This is obtained from bones, cartilage or porkskin. Gelatin is softened in water, dissolved, and added to creams and fillings. You need 2 tbsps of powdered gelatin (or one package) to jell 1 pint of liquid.

Agar-agar

Agar-agar is a vegetarian jelling agent obtained from red seaweed. It is mostly marketed in powder form and has a greater jelling power than gelatin. Agar-agar must not be cooked with dairy products. When using agar-agar, always make sure that the preparation process is concluded quickly – it jells at 86°F.

Gelatin

Agar-agar

SWEETENERS

Cakes, pastries, and cookies taste better when well sweetened. Not only can various types of sugar be used for this, but also honey and molasses, or corn or maple syrup. The spicy flavor of syrup and dark sugars makes them particularly popular for Christmas cookery.

Sugar

In Central Europe, white sugar is obtained from sugar beet, but the best sugar comes from sugar cane, grown mainly in Hawaii, Louisiana, and South America. Various grades of sugar are available on the market.

Granulated and **superfine sugars** are the basic types and the best-value sugars to use.

Confectioner's or **powdered sugar** is finely pulverized, so that the crystals are completely broken up. It is used for dusting and frosting cakes.

Coarse sugar has extra-large crystals produced from refined sugar and is used to decorate buns, cakes, and pastries. It is difficult to find in the U.S.

Brown sugar is partially refined, unbleached raw sugar with a spicy flavor, used mainly for gingerbread and Christmas cakes. There are both light and dark brown varieties.

Rock candy (white or brown) is made by dissolving pure sugar and slowly crystalizing it. For brown rock candy, caramelized sugar is added.

Vanilla sugar is made with ground vanilla beans and refined sugar.

Fruit sugar (or fructose)

This sugar occurs naturally in fruit, vegetables, and fruit

White sugar

Confectioner's sugar

Coarse sugar

Brown sugar

Vanilla sugar

Honey

Maple syrup

Raw cane sugar

juices. Fruit sugar can be used instead of granulated sugar in home baking, causing a deeper browning effect. This white, odorless sugar has a somewhat higher sweetening power than normal sugar, so less need be used. It can be eaten by diabetics, because no insulin is needed to break it down. Diabetics, however,

should take no more than 1 ounce (1 tbsp) at a time and at most 2 ounces (2 tbsps) a day.

Honey

The health-giving properties of honey are frequently questioned. But it is a fact that it consists mainly (up to 80%) of sugar and contains traces of minerals and

vitamins. It can be used instead of sugar in baking, which affects the flavor of the product. The type of flower used to produce the honey may feature on the label, for example, honey from fir, heather, lime, and orange-flower. If the label on the jar just says "honey", this means that no type of flower predominates.

Maple syrup

This syrup is produced mainly in the U.S. and Canada from the sap of the maple tree. It contains nearly 70% sugar. Taste and color depend on the time of harvest. An early harvest yields amber-colored, medium-sweet syrup, while a late harvest can produce one that is nearly black and cloyingly sweet. The harvest stage is denoted by grading from A to D. Normally, Grade A maple syrup is marketed in health-food stores.

Raw cane sugar or **turbinado sugar**

Whole cane juice is clarified and evaporated to produce crystals of sucrose which are centrifuged. The crystals are dissolved, decolorized and recrystalized as white sugar. The product obtained from the liquid molasses residue following the centrifugal process is known as raw cane sugar. Compared with 99.8% pure sucrose, this type of sugar contains large amounts of minerals and B vitamins.

Molasses

Molasses is another by-product of sugar refining. It contains valuable minerals, especially iron, refined from white sugar, as well as 50–70% sucrose. Blackstrap molasses contains even more nutrients. Molasses has about half the sweetening power of white sugar.

APPLE FLAN
WITH CREAM
TOPPING

Basic recipe
Whole-wheat Cookie Crust

FOR THE CRUST:
*2 cups whole-wheat flour
a pinch of salt
2 tbsps sugar or raw cane
    sugar
⅔ cup butter
2–3 tbsps yogurt*

FOR THE FILLING:
*6 tart green apples
juice of 1 lemon
½ cup almonds or walnuts
2 eggs
⅔ cup light cream
6 tbsps sugar*

1. Mix the flour, salt, and sugar in a bowl. Cut the butter into small pieces and stir into the yogurt.
2. Mix the dough with a knife or in a mixer until it is crumbly.
3. Knead quickly by hand into a smooth dough.
4. Press the dough into a jellyroll or baking pan 10–11 inches across. Raise a rim about 1 inch high.
5. Prick the dough in several places and place the pan in the refrigerator for about an hour.
6. Meanwhile peel or thoroughly rinse the apples, quarter, and core them. Cut into thin slices and mix with the lemon juice.
7. Chop the nuts.
8. Beat the egg yolks with cream and sugar until frothy. Beat the egg whites stiffly and fold them in.
9. Arrange the apples on the pastry base, sprinkle with the nuts, and cover with the cream topping. Bake on the middle shelf of a preheated 400°F oven for about 45 minutes or until well browned.

1

2

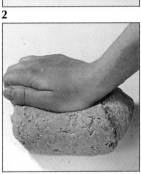

3

4

5

6

7

8

9

Apple Flan

DECORATING
WHOLEFOOD
BAKING

People who are interested in wholefood cooking will naturally avoid elaborate cake decorations such as sugar frosting, chocolate coating, and greasy buttercream fillings. You can decorate cakes and other baked goods with "healthy" ingredients. Julienne strips of untreated lemon peel, for example, are suitable; these can best be made with a julienne cutter or lemon zester. Contrasting colors of nuts can also look pretty, either whole (walnuts, for example) or coarsely chopped (green pistachios).

Cakes, tortes, and gateaux can be easily but effectively decorated with stiffly-whipped cream and a few pieces of fresh fruit or berries.

Instead of chocolate frosting, cakes can be covered with carob coating. This is produced from carob bean flour, oil, milk powder, soya flour, and lecithin and is available in block form. After melting it in a bain-marie, or in the microwave oven on its defrost setting, a metal spatula must be used to spread the softened coating over the cake or cookies, since the coating is too stiff to be applied with a pastry brush.

TIPS ON BAKING

Compared with other types of cookery, baking is a measuring job. All the ingredients must be weighed or measured carefully to ensure that they are in the right proportion to each other. Strictly speaking, a distinction is drawn between a dough and a mixture. Dough is kneaded, and can be rolled out, and pressed or cut into shape before baking. It includes cookie crust, yeast dough, puff and flaky pastry. Mixtures are stirred or beaten; flour and butter, and often whisked egg white too, are carefully combined. Mixtures include, for example, choux paste, sponge cake, and meringue mixtures.

Baking temperatures and times

All recipes give an average temperature and baking time. It takes a little time for the oven to reach the set temperature. If a cake mixture is put into a cold oven the baking time must be prolonged by about 5-10 minutes. When baking in a fan-assisted oven, the temperature must be set about 50°F lower than stated. Cakes take much longer to bake at high altitudes. The food column of your local newspaper can advise of the different baking times.

Shelf height

Deep cakes and pies to be baked in baking pans should be placed on the lowest oven shelf. Flat cakes, such as tarts and flans, should be baked on the middle shelf if not otherwise specified. Cookies mostly require the upper shelf.

Testing

Test a cake by inserting a wooden or metal skewer shortly before the end of the recommended cooking time. If it comes out dry with no mixture clinging to it, then the cake is done. Flat items (cookies, flan cases) are done when they are baked golden-brown.

Guarding against burning

Often the tops of cakes and pies are well browned before their cooking time is up. In this case, just cover the top with nonstick baking parchment and, if possible, turn the top heat off.

After baking

Baked cakes should be left to rest in the pan for about another 5 minutes. Then take them out and let them cool on a cake rack. Loosen cookies from the baking sheet immediately.

Storing cakes

Dry cakes are best kept in a tin or other airtight container. Always put cream gateaux and fruit flans in the refrigerator or at least a cool place, and eat them within 2 days.

Baked goods made with yeast and puff doughs taste far better when eaten fresh.

CREAMED CAKE MIXTURE

Simple waffles, fruit cakes, and tortes can be made with this creamed cake mixture. The basic ingredients remain the same: equal weights of fat, eggs and flour. The sugar can be reduced.

Basic recipe

• Beat together until frothy, 1 cup butter, 1 cup sugar, 2 tbsps vanilla sugar, and a pinch of salt using an electric mixer.

• Add 4 eggs and 1 teaspoon grated lemon rind, a little at a time, and beat into the mixture.

• Sift 2 cups all-purpose flour with ½ tsp baking powder and add to the butter mixture. Finally add 2 tbsps rum or brandy.

• Butter a 1-quart loaf pan, sprinkle it with flour, and fill it with the mixture.

• Bake for 30 minutes at 375°F, then cover with nonstick baking parchment and bake for another 20–25 minutes.

• Shortly before the end of the cooking time, insert a wooden or metal skewer into the center of the cake to see if it is fully baked.

• If the skewer comes out sticky the cake is not yet ready. If the skewer comes out clean the cake is done.

LINING A LOAF PAN WITH BAKING PARCHMENT

1. Draw the outline of the pan onto baking parchment, but somewhat smaller so that it corresponds to the inside measurements.

2. Cut into the 4 corners lengthwise, and cut off just half the paper. Fold the paper inwards along the drawn lines.

3. Fit the folded paper smoothly into the pan. The paper should not protrude more than ½ inch above the rim of the pan.

1

2

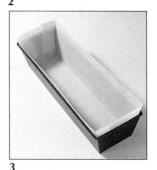

3

SPONGE MIXTURE

Sandwich cakes and jellyrolls need a light sponge mixture. It is most important to whisk the egg whites very stiffly.

Basic recipe

1. Beat 6 egg yolks with 2 tbsps sugar until white and fluffy and increased in volume.

2. Sift 1 cup all-purpose flour and 4 tbsps cornstarch onto a piece of baking parchment.

3. Carefully mix half the flour mixture into the creamed egg and sugar.

4. Whisk the 6 egg whites into stiff peaks, gradually adding in 2 tbsps sugar.

5. Fold a third of the egg white snow into the mixture, then the remaining flour, then the rest of the egg whites.

6. Line or grease a springform pan 10 inches in diameter.

7. Pour the sponge mixture into the cake pan and smooth it flat. Place in a pre-heated oven at 350°F and bake for 30–40 minutes.

8. Place the cooked cake to cool upside down on a floured metal cooling rack.

9. When the cake is cool, unmold it, and slice it into three horizontally.

A chocolate cake can be made in the same way. Simply sift 4 tbsps cocoa powder with the flour and cornstarch.

1

2

3

4

5

6

7

8

9

WHISKING EGG WHITES

In order to ensure that egg whites whisk well and stiffly, the whisk heads and the basin must be completely free of fat. When sugar is added to the egg whites, the snow becomes more solid.

1. Separate the eggs and put the whites into the clean mixing bowl of an electric mixer.

2. Insert the whisk heads and beat the egg whites, slowly at first, then at high speed.

3. The egg whites are fully whisked when they form firm peaks and hold their shape.

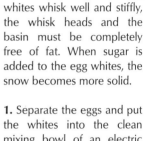

1

2

3

BASIC JELLYROLL

1. Prepare the mixture as before and spread it with a metal spatula to an even thickness on a jellryoll pan lined with nonstick baking parchment. Bake for about 8 minutes in a preheated oven at 475°F.

2. Lay the cooked sponge on a damp cloth and peel off the baking parchment.

3. Lay a second damp cloth over the sponge, weight it down lightly with the pan, and leave to cool.

4. Spread the filling (say, raspberry cream) over the sponge, leaving a good 1-inch margin at the sides so that it will not escape when the cake is rolled up.

5. Use the cloth to help to roll up the sponge, then wrap it in the cloth and leave in the refrigerator to set.

Illustrated here is a jellyroll filled with raspberry cream.

Gateau bases can also be cut out of the sponge sheet.

3

4

5

1

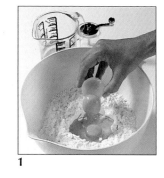

Jellyroll

2

STRUDEL DOUGH

This is easily the most complicated of all doughs to make. Flour, salt, fat, and water must be worked rapidly into a flexible, shiny dough. Thorough beating is also important to remove all air bubbles.

Basic recipe

1. Sift 2½ cups all-purpose flour into a bowl and make a well in the center. Into this put 4 tbsps sunflower oil, 1 egg, 1 egg yolk, ⅔ cup water, and a pinch of salt.

2. Knead the ingredients for at least 10 minutes into a dough that is smooth and elastic, but not sticky. If the dough is too stiff, gradually add a little water.

3. Slap the dough hard on a floured marble or wooden board and shape it into a ball, making sure there are no cracks.

4. Brush the dough with oil and put it in an oiled bowl, cover with plastic wrap, and leave it to rest at room temperature for at least 1 hour.

5. Lightly sprinkle a kitchen towel with flour, roll the dough out on this, and stretch it by hand as thinly as possible.

6. The dough should be teased out over the backs of the hands until wafer-thin.

2

3

4

5

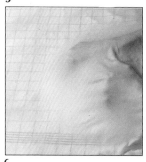

6

1

YEAST DOUGH

No matter whether fresh or dried yeast is used, the method and the result are the same.

Basic recipe

1. Sift 4 cups all-purpose flour into a bowl, make a well in the center, and crumble in 2 tbsps fresh yeast. Sprinkle with 1 tsp sugar and add 1 cup lukewarm milk. Stir to dissolve the yeast in the milk, then mix with some flour to form the starter dough.

2. Sprinkle the starter dough with a little flour, cover with a cloth, and leave it to rise in a warm place for about 20 minutes or until deep cracks appear over the surface.

3. Warm ⅓ cup butter until it melts, then remove from the heat, and add 1 egg and 1 egg yolk. Sprinkle 1 tsp salt over the flour, pour in the butter-and-egg mixture, and stir with a wooden spoon.

4. Squeeze the dough together with your hand and work it until smooth and dry. If it is too stiff, add some milk, if too soft, some water.

5. Shape the light yeast dough into a ball with no cracks. Put it in a basin, cover with a cloth, and leave it to rise for 20–25 minutes.

6. Work the dough again, and leave to rise for a further 20–25 minutes.

2

3

4

5

1

6

COOKIE CRUST

For fruit pies, jam tarts, or sweet pastries, a cookie crust is the ideal base. The high proportion of fat ensures that the dough will be light. The secret of success is to keep all the ingredients as cold as possible.

Basic recipe

1. Heap 2¼ cups sifted all-purpose flour in a ring on the table. Put ¾ cup chilled butter cut in pieces, 3 tbsps sugar, 1 egg, and a pinch of salt in the middle and stir with a knife. Knead the dough rapidly with the hands until it is smooth.

1a. Alternatively put flour, cold butter, and the other ingredients into a mixer and knead with the dough hooks.

2. Shape the dough into a ball, wrap it in plastic wrap, and leave to rest in the refrigerator for at least 1 hour.

3. Roll the dough out, wrap it round a rolling pin, and unroll it over a buttered baking pan.

4. Squeeze the trimmings into a ball and use this to press the dough well into the base and sides of the baking pan.

5. Prick the dough all over with a fork, lay a sheet of baking parchment on it, weighted down with an even sprinkling of dried legumes. Bake in a preheated 400°F oven for about 25 minutes.

1a

2

3

4

1

5

CHOUX PASTE

The high proportion of eggs in the choux puffs it up during cooking.

Basic recipe

1. Boil 1 cup milk, a pinch of salt, a pinch of sugar, with ⅓ cup butter.

2. Sift 2 cups all-purpose flour onto a sheet of kitchen paper. When the milk boils and the butter has melted, take the pan from the heat, pour the flour into it all at once, and beat hard until smooth with a wooden spoon. If the dough is too dry, add a little more milk.

3. Return the pan to the stove over a low heat and beat the mixture until it leaves the bottom of the pan in a single lump.

4. Transfer the mixture to a bowl, let it cool, then beat in 4 eggs, one by one. Do not add another until the previous one is fully incorporated.

5. The choux mixture must be smooth, workable, and of piping consistency.

6. Spoon half the mixture into a pastry bag and pipe puffs and eclairs onto a buttered baking sheet.

7. Place on the center shelf in an oven preheated to 425°F. Place a pan of water in the oven to generate steam that will assist the baking process. Bake for 15–20 minutes.

8. Pipe fritters onto greased nonstick baking parchment.

9. Deep-fry them at about 340°F.

10. The fritters can be glazed with confectioner's sugar if liked.

11. Puffs, eclairs, and fritters are the three most popular types of choux pastries. Puffs and eclairs are filled with a cream filling. Puffs are dusted with confectioner's sugar, eclairs frosted with chocolate or coffee frosting.

LINING A SPRING-FORM PAN

When baking a sponge base, do not grease the sides of the springform pan, as this causes the sponge to stick to it so it cannot shrink away.

1. Cut out a circle of nonstick baking parchment about 2 inches wider than the size of the pan, lay it over the base, and hold it taut with the rim.

2. Place the flan or springform ring on a piece of parchment paper and fold the paper up around the edges so that it sits firmly.

3. Place the pan on a baking sheet and fill with mixture.

FILLING AND ICING A FANCY CAKE OR GATEAU

1. Using a long sharp knife, slice the sponge base horizontally into 3 equal rounds.

2. Lift off the separate rounds, using a cardboard disk or springform base.

3. Coat the bottom layer with cream filling.

4. Place the second layer on top, press down lightly, and spread the filling on this too, then add the third layer and press down.

5. Spread the top and sides of the cake evenly with buttercream.

6. Use a plastic spatula to stick toasted flaked almonds, grated chocolate, or chocolate sprinkles to the sides of the cake.

7. Finally score the cake into slices and use a pastry bag to decorate the top according to taste.

3

4

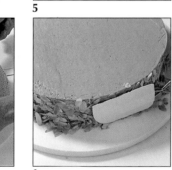

5

1

2

6

7

CONFECTIONER'S CUSTARD

1. Soften a package of gelatin (2 tbsps) in ½ cup cold water. Bring 1 cup milk containing half a split vanilla bean to the boil.

2. Whisk 2 egg yolks with 2 tbsps sugar until pale and creamy. Add the boiling hot milk gradually, while beating.

3. Return the egg and milk to the saucepan and reheat (but do not boil), stirring with a wooden spoon until the mixture thickens and coats the spoon.

4. Dissolve the softened gelatin in the hot vanilla custard. Leave to cool, stirring frequently.

5. Whip 1¼ cups cream until stiff and fold it into the partially-set vanilla custard.

6. A jellyroll can be filled with this custard.

A delicious alternative to confectioner's custard is raspberry cream filling, for both cakes and jellyrolls. To make it, add ⅔ cup raspberry purée and 3 tbsps raspberry liqueur to the cold vanilla custard, and finally fold in 1½ cups stiffly whipped cream. Cream fillings flavored with different fruits can be prepared in the same way.

2

3

4

5

1

Jellyroll with Confectioner's Custard filling

COVERING A CAKE WITH MARZIPAN

1. Knead 1 cup (8 ounces) fresh marzipan quickly with 1 cup confectioner's (powdered) sugar and 1tsp egg white.

2. Sprinkle a marble slab with powdered sugar and roll out the marzipan to the size of the cake.

3. Roll the marzipan round the rolling pin and unroll it over the cake.

4. Press the marzipan firmly onto the cake (with the help of a metal spatula). If any cracks appear, close them with your fingers so that the surface is quite smooth.

5. Paint the marzipan with a thin coat of apricot glaze and leave to dry.

...AND FROSTING

6. Place the cake on a cake stand or a baking sheet. Pour fondant frosting over it.

7. Smooth with a metal spatula or cake knife, so that it is spread thinly and evenly over the top and sides.

8. Fill a paper frosting bag with a different color frosting and squeeze stripes or a spiral over the top.

9. With the back of a cake knife, carefully score lines from the center to the sides of the cake, rinsing the blade after each stroke.

10. A rich or fancy cake is coated with marzipan and frosted.

1

2

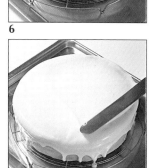

3

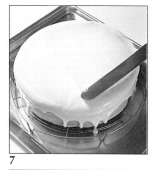

4

5

6

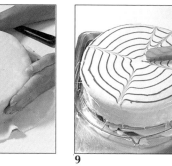

7

8

9

A cake for a special occasion

FRENCH BUTTERCREAM FROSTING

1. Cream 1 cup unsalted butter.

2. Beat together 4 eggs, ⅔ cup sugar, the chopped pulp of a vanilla bean, and a pinch of salt, first over a warm bain-marie, then away from the heat.

3. Slowly beat the egg-and-sugar mixture into the creamed butter. If liked, add some orange juice and grated rind.

Buttercream frosting that is too liquid can be thickened by adding 1 tsp powdered gelatin to 1 cup butter.

1

2

3

GERMAN BUTTERCREAM FROSTING

Fancy cakes filled and frosted with buttercream should not be kept longer than 2 days.

1. Cream ¾ cup unsalted butter at room temperature with 6 tbsps confectioner's sugar.
2. Gradually work in about 2¼ cups confectioner's custard. The custard must not be colder than the butter or it will liquify.
3. This basic buttercream can be flavored according to taste, for example with cocoa powder or a liqueur.

1

2

3

FLAN TOPPING AND APRICOT GLAZE

Colorless or red jelly glaze can be bought in packets and should be used according to the instructions. Instead of water, clear fruit juice or wine can be used. The topping must be spread while over the fruits. Frozen fruits should be glazed with boiling hot topping.

Apricot glaze is a glaze in its own right, but it is mainly used as an insulating layer between a cake and its final frosting. It should always be applied warm.

FRUIT FLAN WITH TOPPING

1. Cover the baked cookie crust base with confectioner's custard.
2. Arrange hulled, washed, and drained strawberries over the top.
3. Pour the warm topping over the fruits and decorate the edge with toasted flaked almonds.
4. When the topping has cooled, decorate the flan with cream rosettes, strawberries, and mint leaves.

1

2

3

4

Strawberry flan

MAKING APRICOT GLAZE

1. Simmer ⅔ cup sugar, ½ cup water, and 2 tbsps lemon juice for 3 minutes, or until the liquid is clear.
2. Rub 1 cup apricot jam through a fine sieve into a pan.
3. Pour the syrup into the jam and simmer for about 10 minutes, stirring constantly. The apricot glaze must be clear and transparent.

Orange marmalade, strawberry, or raspberry jam or jelly can be used instead of apricot jam.

1

2

3

Hearty Home Cooking

As you peruse this chapter the smell of old-fashioned home baking will rise to your nostrils, for here are assembled all the cakes and pastries that form the traditional repertory of the art of high-quality baking. They include Apple Pie, Butter Cake, Prince Regent Gâteau, Dresden Christmas Stollen, and Jellyroll. Special occasion cakes, such as Cream Puffs, Apple Turnovers, Plaited Yeast-cake and, most important, Christmas Fancies, are also included – all of them fun to prepare and delicious to eat.

Cherry Cake
(see recipe on page 32)

POPPYSEED PIE

SERVES 12 ■
*Preparation and cooking
time: 1 hour 45 minutes
Kcal per portion: 515
P = 12g, F = 29g, C = 53g*

BASE:
*2 cups all-purpose flour
1 pinch salt
1 egg
⅔ cup butter
3 tbsps sugar
flour for the work surface*

FILLING:
*2 tbsps raisins
3 cups ground poppyseed
⅔ cup sugar
3 tbsps butter
2¼ cups milk
grated rind of ½ lemon
chopped almonds*

FROSTING:
*1¼ cups confectioner's sugar
1–2 tbsps lemon juice*

Add almonds and raisins to the
poppyseed mixture at the last
minute.

While the pie is still warm, spread
it with the lemon frosting.

1. Line a springform pan with nonstick baking parchment. Put the raisins for the filling to soften in lukewarm water.
2. Sift the flour for the mixture onto a pastry board and mix in the salt. Make a well in the middle and break the egg into it. Cut the butter into small pieces and scatter them on top. Sprinkle with the sugar.
3. Work quickly into a smooth dough, first with two knives, then with the hands. Place the dough in the refrigerator to chill for at least 30 minutes.
4. For the filling, place the poppyseed, sugar, butter, milk, and lemon peel in a saucepan and simmer over a low heat for 10 minutes. Add the drained raisins and the almonds. Leave to cool.
5. Pre-heat the oven to 400°F.
6. Put two-thirds of the dough onto a floured pastry-board or work surface and roll it out, not too thinly. Line the base and sides of the cake pan with it and prick the base all over with a fork.
7. Using a spatula, spread the poppyseed mixture evenly over the pastry base in the pan.
8. Roll out the rest of the dough to the size of the pan and lay it carefully over the poppyseed mixture as a lid. Press the edges firmly together so that the filling is well contained.
9. Bake the pie on the middle shelf of the oven for 50–60 minutes. Take the cooked pie out of the pan and leave it on a wire rack.
10. To make the frosting, stir the confectioner's sugar and lemon juice together until smooth and shining.
11. Frost the pie while still warm.

APPLE PIE

SERVES 12 ■
*Preparation and cooking
time: 1 hour 40 minutes
Kcal per portion: 410
P = 5g, F = 17g, C = 59g*

PASTRY:
*2½ cups all-purpose flour
1 pinch baking powder
1 egg
1 egg yolk
1 cup butter
½ cup sugar
grated rind of 1 lemon
flour for rolling out*

FILLING:
*2 tbsps raisins
8 tart, green apples
¼–½ cup sugar*

TOPPING:
*1½ cups confectioner's sugar
1 tbsp water or rum
few flaked almonds*

1. Line a 10-inch springform pan with nonstick baking parchment.
2. For the dough, mix the flour and baking powder and tip onto a pastry board. Make a well in the middle and put the egg and the egg yolk into it. Cut the chilled butter into lumps and spread them evenly around the flour, then sprinkle the lemon rind on top.
3. Mix first with two knives, then, using both hands, quickly knead to a smooth dough. Leave it to chill in the refrigerator for 30 minutes.
4. For the filling, wash and drain the raisins.
5. Peel, quarter, and core the apples, then slice them wafer thin. Mix with the raisins and sugar.
6. Pre-heat the oven to 400°F.
7. Roll out two-thirds of the dough on a floured board and line the base and sides of the pan with it. Prick the base all over with a fork.
8. Arrange the apple mixture evenly over the dough.
9. Roll the rest of the dough

Peel, quarter, and core the
apples.

out to the same size as the pan and lay it carefully over the fruit as a lid. Squeeze the edges of the lid and sides firmly together so that the fruit is well contained.
10. Bake the apple pie on the middle shelf of the oven for 45–50 minutes.
11. For the topping, stir the confectioner's sugar with the rum or water until smooth and shiny.
12. As soon as the pie comes out of the oven, frost it with the topping, scatter the chopped almonds over it, and leave to cool on a cake rack.
The pie tastes particularly good if eaten lukewarm with vanilla-flavored, sweetened whipped cream.

RED BERRY MERINGUE PIE

SERVES 12

Preparation and cooking time: 1 hour 30 minutes
kcal per portion: 380
P = 5g, F = 12g, C = 42g

PASTRY:
2 cups all-purpose flour
2 egg yolks
⅔ cup butter
½ cup sugar
grated rind of ½ lemon
flour for rolling out

FILLING:
2 cups ripe redcurrants or
*   other red berries*
*   (raspberries, cranberries,*
*   etc.)*
3 egg whites
⅔ cup sugar
2 tsps cornstarch
2 tbsps chopped almonds
breadcrumbs

Ripe redcurrants are easy to strip from their stems.

When the egg white is stiff, fold the berries into the meringue mixture.

Fill the blind-baked pastry case with the berry-and-meringue filling and finish baking.

1. Line a 10-inch cake pan with nonstick baking parchment.
2. To make the dough, sift the flour onto a pastry board, make a well in the middle and add the egg yolk. Flake the chilled butter over the flour and sprinkle with the sugar and grated lemon rind.
3. Mix first with two knives, then, using both hands, quickly knead to a smooth dough. Refrigerate for 30 minutes.
4. Pre-heat the oven to 350°F.
5. To make the filling, strip and wash the redcurrants or other red berries and leave in a sieve to drain.
6. Roll out the dough on a floured board and line the springform pan with it. Prick the pastry base all over with a fork. Bake on the middle shelf of the oven for about 25 minutes or until golden-brown. Remove from the oven.
7. Reduce the heat to 300°F.
8. Whisk the egg whites stiffly. Add the sugar and cornstarch and whisk for another few minutes. Fold the berries carefully into the egg-white mixture.
9. Mix the almonds and breadcrumbs together and scatter over the baked pastry base. Fill with the berry-and-meringue mixture.
10. Finish baking on the middle shelf of the oven for 20 minutes.

CLASSIC CHEESECAKE

SERVES 12

Preparation and cooking time: 2 hours
Kcal per portion: 415
P = 14g, F = 18g, C = 50g

BASE:
2 cups all-purpose flour
1 egg
⅔ cup butter
⅓ cup sugar
grated lemon rind
3 tbsps chopped almonds
flour for rolling out

FILLING:
3 cups small-curd cottage
*   cheese*
3 large eggs
¼ cup butter
¾ cup sugar
grated rind of ½ lemon
⅔ cup sour cream
½ cup cornstarch
1 tsp baking powder
⅔ cup raisins, rinsed and
*   floured*

Thoroughly mix all ingredients for the cheese filling with a hand-held beater.

Spread the cottage cheese mixture over a pre-baked pastry base and cook for a further 40 minutes until done.

1. Line the base of a cake pan with nonstick baking parchment. Drain the cottage cheese in a sieve; finish by pressing in a cloth.
2. For the base, sift the flour onto a pastry board, make a well in the middle, and add the egg yolk. Flake the chilled butter over the flour and sprinkle with the sugar, lemon rind, and almonds.
3. Mix first with two knives, then, using both hands, quickly knead to a smooth dough. Refrigerate for 30 minutes.
4. Pre-heat the oven to 400°F.
5. Roll out the dough on a floured board and line the base and sides of a springform pan with it. Prick the pastry base all over with a fork. Bake on the middle shelf of the oven for 20–25 minutes until pale brown but not fully cooked. Reduce the oven heat to 350°F.
6. For the filling, carefully separate the eggs. Beat the butter, egg yolks, sugar, and lemon rind together until thick and frothy.
7. Beat the cottage cheese until smooth, then add it to the mixture, together with the sour cream, sifted baking powder, flour, and raisins. Stir thoroughly.
8. Whisk the egg whites stiffly and fold into the cottage cheese mixture. Turn the filling into the baked pastry case and smooth the top. Bake on the middle shelf for about 40–50 minutes until golden-brown. Turn off the heat, prop open the oven door, and cool the cake in the oven for 30 minutes before removing. This helps stop the cake from sinking. Loosen from the pan and leave to cool on a cake rack. The cheesecake must be completely cold before it is unmolded from the springform.

PRINCE REGENT GÂTEAU

SERVES 12 ■■

*Preparation and cooking
time: 2 hours 10 minutes
Kcal per portion: 640
P = 7g, F = 35g, C = 75g*

CAKE:
*4 eggs, separated
1 cup sugar
grated rind of ½ lemon
⅔ cup butter
2 cups all-purpose flour,
   sifted
2 tsps baking powder*

FILLING:
*1 cup butter
2 cups confectioner's sugar,
   sifted
3 egg yolks
1 tbsp vanilla sugar
6 squares (6 ounces) baking
   chocolate*

TOPPING:
*2 cups confectioner's sugar
1 tbsp vegetable oil
4 tbsps cocoa powder
3 tbsps water*

butter for the cake pan

1. Line a 10-inch cake pan with nonstick baking parchment.
2. Pre-heat the oven to 350°F.
3. For the cake, beat the egg yolks and sugar together until thick and frothy. Add the lemon rind and melted butter and stir thoroughly. While stirring, add the sifted flour and baking powder, a spoonful at a time. Whisk the egg white very stiffly and add it to the mixture, stirring in the first half and folding in the rest.
4. Spread about one-fifth of the cake mixture in the cake pan and bake on the middle shelf of the oven for 15 minutes. Leave to cool on a cake rack.
5. Line the cake pan again with nonstick baking parchment, spread with some

more mixture, and bake. Continue until you have made 5 or 6 layers of cake.
6. Meanwhile, prepare the filling. Soften the butter and beat it until white and creamy. Add the confectioner's sugar, the egg yolk, and the vanilla sugar, stirring continuously.
Break the chocolate into a small bowl and leave it to melt over a bain-marie. Let it cool a little, then stir it into the cream.
7. Spread the filling on all but one of the cooled cake layers, then pile them carefully one on top of another, keeping the sides straight. Place the plain layer on top.
8. For the topping, stir the confectioner's sugar, vegetable oil, cocoa, and water together in a warmed bowl until smooth and shiny. Using a metal spatula dipped in water, spread the topping over the cake. After the topping has cooled, dip a pointed knife in hot water, and mark out 12 slices so that it will be easier to cut later.

CHERRY CAKE

Photo page 26/27

SERVES 8 ■

*Preparation and cooking
time: 1 hour 30 minutes
Kcal per portion: 270
P = 4g, F = 13g, C = 35g*

*Score the slices with a hot knife
after the topping has cooled.*

*⅓ cup butter
⅓ cup sugar
pinch of salt
grated rind of ½ lemon
2 eggs
1¼ cups all-purpose flour
1 tsp baking powder
sour cherries*

*butter for the pan
confectioner's sugar for
   dusting*

1. Pre-heat the oven to 400°F. Line a 9-inch cake pan with nonstick baking parchment.
2. Put the softened butter, sugar, salt, and lemon rind in a bowl and beat until creamy. Stir in the eggs and the sifted flour and baking powder, alternately, little by little.
3. Pit the cherries.
4. Turn the dough into the cake pan and arrange the cherries on top. Bake on the middle shelf of the oven for 40–45 minutes or until golden. Take the cake out of the pan and leave it to cool on a cake rack. Dust with sifted confectioner's sugar.

Instead of cherries, the cake can be decorated with small, ripe, halved peaches.

PEACH PIE

SERVES 20 ■

*Preparation and cooking
time: 1 hour 10 minutes
Kcal per portion: 230
P = 4g, F = 12g, C = 25g*

BASE:
*1 cup butter
1 cup sugar
juice and grated rind of ½
   lemon
1 tbsp rum
4 eggs
2 cups all-purpose flour
2 tsps baking powder*

TOPPING:
*5 small ripe peaches
4 tbsps confectioner's sugar
1 tbsp rum
½ cup halved almonds
confectioner's sugar for
   dusting*

1. Line a jellyroll or pie pan with nonstick baking parchment.
2. For the base, beat the butter and sugar together. Add the lemon juice and rind, rum, and eggs a little at a time, beating continuously.
3. Combine the flour and baking powder and sift into the mixture. Beat thoroughly, then spread the mixture over the lined jellyroll or pie pan.
4. Pre-heat the oven to 400°F.
5. For the topping, stick each peach on a fork and dip into hot water, then skin, halve, pit, and quarter it.
6. Sprinkle the quarters with confectioner's sugar and rum and let them marinade for a short time.
7. Arrange the fruit, cut-side downward, on top of the cake mixture and sprinkle with the almonds.
8. Bake the cake on the middle shelf of the oven for 35 minutes or until golden-brown. Leave to cool, then dust with confectioner's sugar.

BUTTER AND CRUMBLE CAKES

SERVES 12
Preparation and cooking time: 1 hour 20 minutes
Rising time: 2 hours
Kcal per portion: 370
P = 6g, F = 18g, C = 40g

YEAST DOUGH:
4 cups all-purpose flour
1 tsp salt
3 tbsps fresh yeast or 1 package dry yeast
1 cup lukewarm milk
½ cup butter
1 egg
grated rind of ½ lemon
2 tbsps sugar
½ cup raisins
flour for rolling out

BUTTER TOPPING:
1¼ cups butter
¾ cup sugar
1 tsp ground cinnamon
flaked almonds
or

CRUMBLE TOPPING:
1¾ cups all-purpose flour
1 cup sugar
1 cup butter
pinch of ground cinnamon

1. Line a jellyroll pan with nonstick baking parchment.
2. For the dough, mix the salt with the flour in a bowl and make a well in the middle. Crumble the yeast into this and mix it to a starter dough with half the milk and 2 tbsps of the flour. Cover and leave in a warm place for about 15 minutes.
3. Melt the butter in the rest of the milk.
4. Work the starter into a smooth dough with the rest of the ingredients, except the raisins, and knead until it comes away cleanly from the bowl. Knead the raisins into the dough by hand. Cover and leave to rise in a warm place for 1 hour.
5. Roll out the risen dough to fit the pan. Transfer it to the pan and pinch up a rim round the edge. Cover, and leave for 30 minutes.

Scatter flakes of butter over the yeast dough and sprinkle with the sugar-and-cinnamon mixture.

Spread the crumble mixture as evenly as possible over the dough.

6. Pre-heat the oven to 400°F.
7. For the butter topping, use your forefinger to poke evenly-spaced hollows in the dough. Scatter the butter all over the dough in small flakes. Mix the sugar and cinnamon and sprinkle over the dough, with the flaked almonds. Bake on the middle shelf of the oven for about 20–25 minutes or until golden-brown.
8. For the crumble topping, mix the flour, sugar, melted butter, and cinnamon and rub together until crumbly. Spread over the dough as evenly as possible. Bake for a further 20–25 minutes or until golden-brown.

MARBLE CAKE

SERVES 16
Preparation and cooking time: 1 hour 30 minutes
Kcal per portion: 275
P = 5g, F = 14, C = 30

1 cup butter
1 cup sugar
1 tbsp vanilla sugar
4 eggs, separated
2½ cups all-purpose flour
2 tsps baking powder
6 tbsps milk
2 tbsps chopped almonds
3 tbsps cocoa powder or 3½ ounces grated baking chocolate
2 tbsps rum or water

butter and cookie or zwieback crumbs for the pan
confectioner's sugar for dusting

1. Butter a tube pan or Bundt pan and sprinkle it with cookie crumbs.
2. Put the softened butter, sugar, and vanilla sugar into a bowl and beat until creamy. Beat in the egg yolks one by one. Beat in the sift-

> **TIP**
>
> *Using the same recipe you can make a fruit cake. Omit the chocolate and add ½ cup raisins and ¼ cup currants to the mixture.*

ed flour and baking powder, the milk, and the almonds alternately, a little at a time. Whisk the egg whites until stiff, beat half of the foam into the mixture, and fold in the rest.
3. Pre-heat the oven to 375°F.
4. Put a third of the mixture into a separate bowl and mix in the cocoa or grated chocolate, and the rum or water.

Spoon the chocolate mixture over the pale mixture.

Swirl the two colors together using a fork.

5. Put the white mixture into the cake pan first, and then carefully pour the chocolate mixture on top. Swirl the two colors together to create a marble pattern, using a fork.
6. Place on the bottom shelf of the oven and bake for 60–70 minutes. Test with a skewer to see if the cake is done; if not, bake for a further 10 minutes.
7. Leave the cake to cool for 15 minutes, then turn it out onto a rack, and dust with confectioner's sugar. It is best left until the next day before cutting.

CREAM PUFFS

SERVES 24 ■

*Preparation and cooking
time: 1 hour
Kcal per portion: 135
P = 3g, F = 10g, C = 10g*

DOUGH:
*1 cup water
4 tbsps butter
pinch of salt
1¼ cups all-purpose flour
4-5 eggs*

FILLING:
*2 cups double or whipping
   cream
1 tbsp sugar
1 tbsp vanilla sugar
confectioner's sugar for
   dusting*

1. Line a baking sheet with nonstick baking parchment. Pre-heat the oven to 500°F.
2. For the choux paste, put the water, butter, and salt into a pan, bring to the boil, and tip the flour all at once into the boiling liquid. Lower the heat and stir until the ball of dough loosens from the bottom of the pan. Remove from heat and beat the eggs into the mixture, one at a time.
3. Using two teaspoons, arrange walnut-sized heaps of choux paste on the baking sheet. Place on the middle shelf of the oven and bake for about 30 minutes or until golden-brown. Use scissors to cut the puffs open straight away.
4. For the filling, beat the cream with sugar and vanilla sugar until stiff. When the puffs are cold, fill them and close them again, then dust with confectioner's sugar. The same mixture can be used to make éclairs, filled with whipped cream and frosted with coffee or chocolate-flavored frosting.

JELLYROLL

SERVES 8 ■

*Preparation and cooking
time: 45 minutes
Cooling time: 30 minutes
Kcal per portion: 415
P = 8g, F = 19g, C = 54g*

SPONGE:
*4 eggs, separated
4 tbsps warm water
¾ cup sugar
grated rind of ½ lemon
1 cup all-purpose flour
3 tbsps cornstarch
1 tsp baking powder*

FILLING:
*3 cups ripe strawberries
½ cup sugar
1½ cups double or whipping
   cream
1 tbsp powdered gelatin*

1. Line a jellyroll pan with nonstick baking parchment.
2. For the sponge, put the egg yolks in a bowl with the water, sugar, and lemon rind and beat until thick and creamy.
3. Mix together the flour, cornstarch, and baking powder, sift into the egg mixture, and carefully fold in with a wooden spatula.
4. Pre-heat the oven to 375°F.
5. Beat the egg whites very stiffly and use the whisk to fold them into the mixture. Do not stir too vigorously.
6. Use a spatula to spread the mixture over the prepared pan. Bake on the middle shelf of the oven for 12–15 minutes or until golden.
7. For the filling, rinse and hull the strawberries and drain well on kitchen paper. Halve or quarter large fruit. Mix in a basin with 2 tbsps sugar. Reserve a few particularly fine strawberries.
8. After baking, turn the sponge out immediately onto a damp, well wrung-out tea towel, peel off the paper and roll up the sponge with the help of the cloth.

Roll up the still warm sponge with the help of a damp kitchen towel.

Unroll the sponge when cooled, fill with strawberry cream, and roll up again.

9. Whip the cream until stiff. Dissolve the gelatin in 2–3 tbsps hot water. Cool it slightly and mix with the remaining sugar.
10. Reserve one third of the cream and mix the rest with the drained and sugared strawberries.
11. Unroll the cooled sponge on the tea towel, spread it with strawberry cream, and roll it up again.
12. Spread cream thinly over the outside of the roll. Place the rest of the cream in a piping bag and decorate the roll. Add the final touch with the reserved strawberries and leave the finished cake for 30 minutes in the refrigerator.

BRAIDED YEAST-CAKE

SERVES 15 ■

*Preparation and cooking
time: 1 hour
Rising time: about 2 hours
Kcal per portion: 195
P = 5g, F = 5g, C = 32g*

*4 cups all-purpose flour
1 tsp salt
1 tbsp fresh yeast
1 cup lukewarm milk
2 tbsps sugar
¼ cup butter
grated rind of 1 lemon
1 egg*

*flour for rolling out
1 egg yolk for brushing
sugar sprinkles for decorating*

1. Line a baking sheet with nonstick baking parchment.
2. Mix the flour and salt in a bowl. Make a well in the middle. Crumble in the yeast and mix to a starter dough with half the milk, 1 tsp sugar, and 2 tbsps flour. Cover and leave to rise in a warm place for 20 minutes.
3. Work the rest of the ingredients into a smooth dough and continue to beat until the mixture leaves the sides of the bowl. Cover and leave to rise in a warm place for 1–1½ hours.
4. Turn the dough onto a floured board and cut into three. Form each of the three pieces into a long roll and braid them together. Turn the ends under.
5. Lay the braid on the baking sheet, brush with egg yolk, sprinkle, with sugar sprinkles and leave to rise again for about 20 minutes.
6. Pre-heat the oven to 400°F.
7. Bake the braid on the middle shelf of the oven for 40–45 minutes or until golden-brown.

APPLE TURNOVERS

SERVES 16
Preparation and cooking time: 1 hour 30 minutes
Kcal per portion: 145
P = 3g, F = 9g, C = 13g

PASTRY:
1 cup all-purpose flour
1 egg yolk
⅔ cup small curd cottage cheese
1 pinch salt
½ cup butter

FILLING:
ripe apples
2 tbsps sugar
2 tbsps rum or kirsch
grated rind of ½ lemon
2 tbsps coarsely chopped almonds
1 tbsp raisins

flour for rolling out
1 egg white for brushing

1. Line a baking sheet with nonstick baking parchment.
2. For the dough, sift the flour onto a pastry board, make a well in the middle, and add the egg yolk, cheese, and salt. Flake the chilled butter and scatter it all over the flour.
3. Quickly knead all the ingredients into a smooth dough. Leave the dough in the refrigerator for 30 minutes.

TIP

This quickly prepared cottage cheese puff pastry is equally suitable for savory fillings. The pastries should be eaten on the day they are made.

4. For the filling, peel, halve and core the apples and rub them through a coarse grater.

Mix the ingredients for the filling well and flavor with rum or kirsch.

Fold the circles of dough over the filling and bend them into crescents.

5. Flavor the apples with sugar, rum, or kirsch, and lemon rind; stir in the almonds and raisins.
6. Pre-heat the oven to 400°F.
7. Roll the dough into a rectangle on a floured board and fold the two ends to the middle. Roll out again and repeat the process at least twice more. Three times is even better. Finally roll the pastry out to the thinness of the back of a knife-blade. Using a round 4-inch cookie cutter (or a glass), cut out 16 circles of dough.
8. Place a tablespoon of apple filling on each circle. Brush the edges with egg white and fold the circles over into half-moon shapes.
9. Arrange the apple turnovers on the baking sheet and bake on the middle shelf of the oven for 20 minutes or until golden.

SPICED ALMOND COOKIES

MAKES ABOUT 40
Preparation and cooking time: 1 hour 15 minutes
Kcal per portion: 140
P = 2g, F = 8g, C = 16g

4 cups all-purpose flour
1 tbsp baking powder
2 eggs
1 cup butter
1 cup sugar
1½ cups ground almonds
some grated lemon rind
1 tsp cinnamon
pinch of ground cloves
small pinch of ground cardamom
1 tsp cocoa powder
flour for rolling out

1. Line a baking sheet with nonstick baking parchment.
2. Sift the flour with the baking powder and heap it on a pastry board. Make a well in the middle and break in the eggs. Flake the chilled butter all over the flour. Sprinkle with the sugar, lemon rind, cinnamon, cloves, cardamom, and cocoa.
3. Using first two knives, then your two hands, knead to a smooth dough. Leave the dough for 30 minutes in the refrigerator.
4. Pre-heat the oven to 400°F.
5. Roll the dough out thinly on a floured board or worktop. Flour fluted cookie cutters and press out the shapes. Trim any excess with a sharp knife.
6. Arrange the spiced cookies on the baking sheet and bake on the middle shelf of the oven for 15 minutes or until golden.

VANILLA CROISSANTS

MAKES ABOUT 40
Preparation and cooking time: 1 hour 30 minutes
Kcal per portion: 105
P = 2g, F = 7g, C = 10g

2½ cups all-purpose flour
2 egg yolks
1 cup butter
⅔ cup ground almonds
½ cup sugar

sugar for sprinkling
flour for dusting
4 tbsps confectioner's sugar, flavored with vanilla bean

1. Line a baking sheet with nonstick baking parchment.
2. Heap the flour on a pastry board or worktop, make a well in the middle, and add the egg yolk. Flake the chilled butter all over the flour and sprinkle with the almonds and sugar.
3. First with two knives, then with your two hands, knead to a smooth dough. Wrap the dough in foil and leave in the refrigerator for 30 minutes.
4. Pre-heat the oven to 350°F.
5. With lightly-floured hands, shape small croissants from the pastry, arrange them on the baking sheet, and bake on the middle shelf of the oven for 20–25 minutes until golden.
6. While still warm, toss the croissants in the vanilla-flavored confectioner's sugar and store in an airtight container in layers separated by wax paper.

DRESDEN CHRISTMAS STOLLEN

SERVES 24 ■■

*Preparation and cooking
time: 2 hours
Rising time: 30 minutes
Resting time: several hours,
preferably overnight
Kcal per portion: 505
P = 8g, F = 26g, C = 60g*

*10 cups all-purpose flour
1 tsp salt
3 tbsps fresh yeast or 1
    package dried yeast
1 cup lukewarm milk
1 cup butter
⅔ cup lard or suet
⅔ cup sugar
2 egg yolks
grated rind of 1 lemon
2 cups almonds
¼ tsp almond-extract
5 tbsps candied lemon peel
2 cups raisins
⅔ cup butter for brushing
1¼ cups confectioner's sugar
    for dusting*

1. Mix the flour and salt together in a bowl, make a well in the middle and crumble in the yeast. Mix to a starter dough with half the milk and some of the flour. Cover and leave to rise in a warm place for 30 minutes.
2. Melt the butter and lard or suet in the rest of the milk, and add to the dough. Add the sugar, egg yolk, and grated lemon rind and mix to a smooth dough. Work it until it no longer sticks to the bowl. Leave to rise in a warm place for at least 1 hour.
3. Meanwhile, blanch the almonds in boiling water, skin them, and chop roughly. Cut the candied lemon peel finely and rinse the raisins.
4. Knead the almonds, candied peel, and raisins into the dough. Roll out to a circle, then fold both sides inward, one on top of the other, to form a loaf shape. Press lightly.

Fold the dough over into the typical stollen shape.

The warm butter seals the pores of the loaf, thereby enabling the stollen to be stored for a long time.

5. Leave the stollen to rest for several hours, preferably overnight.
6. Pre-heat the oven to 375°F some 5 to 10 minutes beforehand. Line a baking sheet with nonstick baking parchment.
7. Place the stollen on the baking sheet and bake on the bottom shelf of the oven for 1¼–1½ hours or until well browned. Test with a skewer to make sure it is done.
8. Melt the butter in a pan. Put the baked Stollen on a rack. While still warm, brush it with half the butter and sprinkle it with half the confectioner's sugar. Repeat after 5 minutes.

NUREMBERG LEBKUCHEN

SERVES 15 ■

*Preparation and cooking
time: 1 hour
Resting time: overnight
Kcal per portion: 325
P = 7g, F = 11g, C = 50g*

DOUGH:
*4 eggs
1 cup sugar
2 cups blanched almonds,
    finely chopped
1 tsp whole mace
1 tsp ground cardamom
1 tsp ground cinnamon
½ tsp ground cloves
grated rind of ½ lemon
2 tbsps each of finely chopped
    candied lemon peel and
    orange peel
2 cups all-purpose flour
1 tsp baking powder
15 round rice-paper wafers*

FROSTING:
*1¼ cups confectioner's sugar
1–2 tbsps lemon juice
chocolate or sugar sprinkles
    for decorating*

1. For the dough, beat together the eggs and sugar until thick and frothy. Add the almonds, spices, and candied peel and sift in the flour and baking powder.
2. Arrange the wafers on the baking sheet. Spread each with the mixture, half a finger thick. Leave to stand overnight.
3. Pre-heat the oven to 350°F.
4. Bake the lebkuchen on the middle shelf of the oven for 20–25 minutes. While still warm, brush with frosting and sprinkle some colored sugar or chocolate sprinkles on the center of each.

SWEET SHORTCRUST STARS

MAKES ABOUT 25 ■

*Preparation and cooking
time: 1 hour
Kcal per portion: 170
P = 2g, F = 9g, C = 20g*

*2½ cups all-purpose flour
1 cup butter
½ cup sugar
6 tbsps unblanched ground
    almonds
pinch ground cloves
pinch cinnamon
pinch ground cardamom
flour for rolling out
1 cup confectioner's sugar for
    dusting
½ cup jam for decorating*

1. Line a baking sheet with nonstick baking parchment.
2. Heap the flour on a pastry board and scatter over it the chilled, flaked butter, sugar, almonds, and spices.
3. Mix first with two knives, then using both hands, quickly knead to a smooth dough. Leave in a cold place for 30 minutes.
4. Pre-heat the oven to 350°F.
5. Roll the dough out on a floured board to ⅒-inch thick and cut out stars using a star-shaped cookie cutter. In half the stars cut a small hole in the middle.
6. Arrange the stars on the baking sheet and bake on the middle shelf for 10–15 minutes until golden.
7. Dust the stars with the holes with confectioner's sugar, and spread jam in the middle of the others. Place the sugared stars over the jam-coated ones, taking care that the points coincide.

Cakes from Around the World

*T*his section contains sweet delights from the ovens of countries around the world and illustrated with their recipes. You can transport yourself in spirit on journeys all over the globe and sample typical food from many distant regions. Offerings include Battenberg Cake from England and Dundee cake from Scotland; Puff Pastries with Lemon Cream from France; and the traditional cakes of Europe are also represented in Basque Cake and Swedish Tosca Cake. The rich cornucopia of international baking reaches even as far afield as Turkey, Haiti, and Arabia.

Arabian Almond Vol-au-vents
(see recipe on page 52)

ENGADINE
NUT PIE

ENGADINE NUT PIE

SERVES 12　▪▪

Preparation and cooking time: 1 hour
Resting time: 1 hour
Kcal per portion: 765
P = 10g, F = 44g, C = 81g

PASTRY:
1 cup butter
¾ cup sugar
grated rind of 1 lemon
2 eggs
1 tbsp rum
4 cups all-purpose flour

FILLING:
1½ cups filberts (hazelnuts)
1⅓ cups sugar
1 cup heavy cream
3 tbsps honey
1 tbsp rum

butter for the pan
flour for rolling out
1 egg yolk for brushing

The ingredients for the pastry are best blended in a food processor.

Top the nut filling with pastry and garnish with pastry shapes.

1. For the dough, soften the butter and beat until creamy with the sugar and lemon rind. Add the eggs and rum in turn, beating all the time.

> **TIP**
>
> *Alternatively, the pie can be topped with a lattice of pastry strips.*

Beat in the sifted flour a little at a time. Leave the dough in the refrigerator for 1 hour.
2. For the filling, chop the filberts coarsely. Toast the sugar in a heavy pan until light yellow, add the nuts, and briefly toast together. Pour in the cream, allow to heat through, then add the honey and rum. Leave to cool.
3. Pre-heat the oven to 400°F. Line the base of a 10-inch springform pan with nonstick baking parchment.
4. Cut the dough into three. Roll one third out on a floured pastry board and line the base of the cake pan with it. Prick the pastry base all over with a fork. Make the next piece into a roll, lay it round the edge of the pan, and use a fork to press it against the base. Spread the filling over the pastry base. Roll the third piece out into a lid for the pie, lay it in place, and press down the edges. Use any leftovers to make shapes to decorate to taste. Brush the top with egg yolk and bake on the middle shelf of the oven for 45 minutes, or until browned.
5. Bake the pie a day before eating – it must set firm before it can be sliced. It will keep for quite a long time.

FRENCH PEAR TART

Tarte aux poires et aux amandes

SERVES 8　▪▪

Preparation and cooking time: 1 hour
Resting time: 1 hour
Kcal per portion: 525
P = 8g, F = 26g, C = 63

PASTRY:
2 cups all-purpose flour
1 tbsp sugar
tsp salt
⅔ cup butter
4 tbsps water
flour for rolling out

TOPPING:
2 pounds pears
1 cup water
1 piece of vanilla bean
¾ cup sugar

ALMOND CREAM:
1 cup almonds
⅔ cup confectioner's sugar
2 eggs
2 tbsps double cream
2 tbsps pear liqueur or rum

1. For the dough, mix the flour, sugar, and salt in a basin. Scatter the chilled butter over it in small flakes. Add the cold water then work with the hands into a smooth dough.
2. Shape the dough into a ball and wrap in aluminum foil. Leave in a cool place for about an hour.
3. For the topping, peel, halve, and core the pears.
4. Heat the water in a pan with the vanilla bean and sugar, and reduce to a syrup. Cook the pears in this until transparent but not too soft. Lift them out of the liquid with a slotted spoon and drain on a sieve.
5. Boil the pear syrup until thick.
6. Pre-heat the oven to 400°F. Line a 9-inch springform pan with nonstick baking parchment.

Cook the pear halves in the syrup until transparent but not too soft.

After baking, brush the tart with reduced pear syrup.

7. For the cream, blanch the almonds, then grind them finely, and mix with the sifted confectioner's sugar.
8. Whisk the eggs until frothy. Add the cream and alcohol and whisk together. Finally stir in the almond mixture.
9. Roll the dough out on a floured board and line the base and sides of a greased and floured springform pan with it. Prick the pastry base all over with a fork. Bake on the middle shelf of the oven for 15 minutes.
10. Spread the almond cream on the pastry base and lay the pear halves over it in a star pattern. Return to the oven and bake for a further 25 minutes.
11. Glaze the top of the cooked tart with the pear syrup.

HAITIAN COCONUT PUDDING

Gâteau de coco à la haitienne

SERVES 12 ■ ■
Preparation and cooking time: 1 hour 45 minutes
Kcal per portion: 515
P = 9g, F = 25g, C = 61g

12 slices of white bread
1 cup softened butter
1 cup passion fruit
   (granadilla) or pineapple
   jam
3 cups milk
4 egg yolks
2 tbsps sugar
good pinch of grated nutmeg
pulp of vanilla bean
pinch of cinnamon
½ cup raisins, soaked in 4
   tbsps rum
4 tbsps shredded coconut

MERINGUE TOPPING:
4 egg whites
¾ cup sugar
½ cup shredded coconut

butter for the pan

Sprinkle raisins, rum, and shredded coconut over the buttered and jam-spread bread.

Heap the meringue thickly over the last layer of bread.

1. Line a deep pie pan or springform pan about 9 inches in diameter with aluminum foil, and butter generously.
2. Spread the bread with three-quarters of the butter. Spread jam on 8 slices.
3. Bring the milk to the boil. Beat the egg yolk with the sugar and spices until frothy and, still beating, pour in the hot milk.
4. Line the pan with 4 jam slices. Sprinkle with half the drained raisins, half the rum, and half the shredded coconut, and cover with another 4 of the jam slices.
5. Sprinkle with the rest of the raisins, rum, and coconut and cover with the remaining, plain bread-and-butter. Slowly pour on the egg-and-milk so that it is completely absorbed by the bread.

6. Pre-heat the oven to 375°F.
7. For the meringue topping, whisk the egg whites very stiffly, add the sugar, and continue whisking until creamy. Then fold in the shredded coconut.
8. Heap the meringue thickly over the bread and use a spoon to raise it in little peaks.
9. Bake the pudding on the bottom shelf for about 40 minutes or until golden.

Serve as a dessert accompanied by a fruit sauce of freshly puréed berries with sugar.

PUFF PASTRIES WITH LEMON CREAM

Millefeuille au citron

MAKES 12 ■
Preparation and cooking time: 1 hour 15 minutes
Cooling time: 30 minutes
Kcal per portion: 310
P = 4g, F = 22g, C = 24g

2 x 9-ounce packages of
   frozen puff dough

LEMON CREAM:
4 eggs
½ cup softened butter
¾ cup sugar
grated rind of 1 lemon
juice of 4 lemons
1¼ cups heavy cream
confectioner's sugar for
   dusting

For the lemon cream, squeeze the 4 lemons and mix with all the other ingredients except the cream.

Use a whisk to stir the whipped cream into the cooled lemon cream.

Sandwich the lemon cream between the puff pastry bases.

1. Leave the puff pastry to thaw for 20 minutes.
2. Line the bases of two 8-inch springform pans with nonstick baking parchment.
3. Pre-heat the oven to 425°F.
4. Roll out the thawed dough and cut it into four circles to fit the springform pans. Place one in each pan and put them into the oven side-by-side on the middle shelf. Bake for 15 minutes or until golden-brown. Release them from the pans and leave to cool on a rack. Do the same with the other two pastry bases.
5. For the lemon cream, put all the ingredients except the cream in a heavy-bottomed pan (or a basin in a bain-marie) and whisk together thoroughly. Constantly whisk over a low heat until a thickish cream is produced. Remove the pan from the heat and cool the basin in ice-cold water, stirring the mixture occasionally.
6. Whip the cream stiffly and fold it into the lemon cream.
7. Spread three of the pastry bases with the cream, pile them on top of each other and top with the fourth base. Dust the top with confectioner's sugar. Refrigerate for about 30 minutes before serving.

The cake can be thinly frosted with a lemon frosting.

BASQUE CAKE

Gâteau basque

SERVES 12 ■
*Preparation and cooking
time: 1 hour 15 minutes
Cooling time: 1 hour
Kcal per portion: 425
P = 7g, F = 20g, C = 52g*

FILLING:
2 egg yolks
3 tbsps sugar
2 tbsps all-purpose flour
1 cup milk
4 tbsps ground almonds
1 tbsp rum

PASTRY:
3½ cups all-purpose flour
2 tsps baking powder
2 egg yolks
1 egg
1 cup butter
1 cup sugar
4 tsps armagnac
grated rind of 1 lemon

flour for rolling out
1 egg yolk for brushing

*Thicken the cream over a low
heat then allow to cool, stirring
constantly.*

*Cover the filled base with the
pastry lid and press the edges of
the pastry together.*

1. Line the base of a 9-inch springform pan with nonstick baking parchment.
2. For the filling, beat the egg yolk into the sugar and add the flour. Boil the milk and beat it in a little at a time, followed by the almonds and rum.
3. Pour the cream into a saucepan, place it over a low heat, and stir constantly until thick, then allow to cool, stirring occasionally.
4. For the pastry, sift the flour and baking powder onto a pastry board, make a well in the middle, and add the egg yolks and the egg. Flake the chilled butter all over the flour and sprinkle with the sugar, armagnac, and lemon rind.
5. Work rapidly to a smooth dough, first using two knives then both hands. Shape into a ball and leave in the refrigerator for 1 hour.
6. Pre-heat the oven to 400°F.

7. Divide the dough into two, and roll out two bases on a floured pastry board, one of them a little larger than the springform base. Lay this larger one in the pan and add a small rim. If the dough should split (being very soft and fragile), carefully press it together again. Prick the base all over with a fork.
8. Spread the cream over the base and cover with the other half. Press the edges of the two pastry layers together and brush with egg yolk.
9. Bake the cake on the middle shelf of the oven for 35-40 minutes or until golden-brown.

BATTENBERG CAKE

SERVES 10 ■ ■
*Preparation and cooking
time: 1 hour 10 minutes
Cooling time: 1-2 hours
Kcal per portion: 655
P = 9g, F = 32g, C = 83g*

1 cup butter
1 cup sugar
4 eggs
1 tbsp rum
2 cups all-purpose flour
1 tbsp vanilla sugar
2 tbsps cocoa
1 tbsp milk
1 cup apricot jam
10 ounces marzipan
1 egg white
6 tbsps confectioner's sugar
confectioner's sugar for
    rolling out

1. Line two small loaf pans 8 inches long with nonstick baking parchment. Pre-heat the oven to 375°F.
2. Put the softened butter and the sugar in a basin and beat until creamy. Beat in the eggs and rum and add the flour.
3. Divide the mixture in half. Mix one half with the vanilla sugar and the other with the cocoa and milk. Put each half in a loaf pan and bake on the middle shelf of the oven for 40 minutes or until done. Remove from the oven, allow to cool slightly in the pans then turn them out onto a cake rack.
4. When the cakes have cooled completely, cut them straight across, then lengthwise into four even strips. Arrange the brown and white strips alternately, four abreast and four deep, sticking them together with hot apricot jam.
5. Knead the marzipan with the egg white and the confectioner's sugar and roll out on confectioner's sugar to the size of the cake. Brush the cake with apricot jam and wrap it in the marzipan.

*Bake one dark and one light cake
in loaf pans.*

*Lay the strips together, brushing
them with apricot jam.*

*Brush the entire cake with jam
and wrap in marzipan.*

Leave 1–2 hours before slicing. Unsliced, Battenberg Cake will keep for several days.

SWEDISH TOSCA CAKE

Toscakaka

SERVES 8

*Preparation and cooking
time: 1 hour
Kcal per portion: 395
P = 6g, F = 24g, C = 38g*

CAKE:
*2 eggs
⅔ cups sugar
1 ⅓ cups all-purpose flour
1 tsp baking powder
½ cup melted butter
2 tbsps milk or cream
butter and zwieback crumbs
   for the pan*

CARAMEL TOPPING:
*4 tbsps butter
4 tbsps split almonds
2 tbsps sugar
1 tbsp flour
1 tbsp milk or cream*

1. Grease an 8-inch spring-form pan and sprinkle with zwieback crumbs. Pre-heat the oven to 350°F.
2. For the cake, beat the eggs and sugar together until frothy. Carefully fold in the sifted flour and baking powder. Lastly, stir in the melted butter and milk or cream.
3. Put the mixture in the pan and bake on the middle shelf of the oven for 30 minutes.
4. For the caramel topping, melt the butter and add the split almonds, sugar, flour, and milk or cream. Cook gently for 5 minutes.
5. After the 30 minutes baking time, take the cake out of the oven, pour the caramel topping over it, and bake for a further 15 minutes or until golden-brown.
6. Take the cake from the oven, let it cool in the pan, and then stand on a cake rack until cold enough for cutting.

CHINESE DATE PANCAKES

**MAKES 12 SMALL
PORTIONS**

*Preparation and cooking
time: 1 hour
Kcal per portion: 210
P = 2g, F = 13g, C = 21g*

MIXTURE:
*1 cup all-purpose flour
1 egg
1 cup water
oil for frying*

FILLING:
*¾ cup pitted dates
2 tbsps lard
1 tbsp sugar*

1. For the pancake mixture, put the flour in a basin, make a well in the middle, and break in the egg. Beat in the egg and slowly add the water until a smooth pancake mixture is obtained.
2. For the filling, put the dates in a pan, cover well with water, and simmer until the fruit is completely soft. Strain, reserving the date cooking water. Press the fruit through the sieve, leaving the skins behind. Add sufficient date cooking water to make a thick paste.
3. Heat the lard in a wok. Add the sugar and stir until dissolved. Then add the date paste and cook until a thick, dry paste is obtained. Allow to cool a little.
4. Grease a large wok with some oil, pour the batter in and, over maximum heat, fry a large, thin pancake. Leave to cool.
5. Spread the date paste over the pancake, leaving a margin, and roll up. Mix some flour and water to a paste and use it to seal the openings.
6. Wipe the wok with kitchen paper, heat it on the stove, and pour in a little oil.

Pit the dates and cook in water until soft.

Spread the date paste on a large thin pancake and roll it up.

Allow the fried date roll to cool a little before slicing.

Fry the roll and remove from the pan.
7. Put a little more oil in the wok and heat it until very hot. Add the date roll and fry for about 1 minute until crisp. Remove and cool. Before serving, cut into 12 slices.

DUNDEE CAKE

SERVES 20

*Preparation and cooking
time: 2 hours 30 minutes
Kcal per portion: 280
P = 4g, F = 14g, C = 33g*

*1 cup butter
1 cup brown sugar
4 eggs
2 cups all-purpose flour
½ tsp baking powder
2 tbsps ground almonds
1 cup raisins
⅔ cup currants
1 tbsp chopped candied
   lemon peel
1 tbsp chopped candied
   orange peel
2 tbsps candied cherries,
   quartered*

*butter for the pan
flour for the fruit
½ cup blanched and
   halved almonds for
   decoration*

1. Line the base and sides of a 9-inch cake pan with non-stick baking parchment, letting the paper stand twice as high as the sides of the pan. Butter the paper well.
2. Beat the butter and sugar together until creamy. Add the eggs, the sifted flour, and baking powder, and the almonds little by little, alternately.
3. Lightly flour the raisins, currants, finely chopped lemon and orange peel, and quartered cherries, and add to the mixture.
4. Pre-heat the oven to 325°F.
5. Put the mixture in the pan, smooth the top, and decorate with a circle of almonds.
6. Bake the cake on the bottom shelf of the oven for 1¾ to 2 hours. If the top of the cake is getting too dark, cover it with nonstick baking parchment.
7. Let the cake cool, remove from the tin and peel off the paper.

TURKISH PASTRIES

Baklava

MAKES 24 ■ ■ ■
*Preparation and cooking
time: 2 hours 30 minutes
Kcal per portion: 320
P = 5g, F = 17g, C = 36g*

PASTRY:
*4 cups all-purpose flour
2 tbsps oil
pinch of salt
1 egg
1 cup lukewarm water*

FILLING:
*1 cup shelled walnuts
1 cup shelled almonds
½ cup shelled pistachios
½ cup sugar
1 cup butter for brushing*

SYRUP:
*1 cup water
1⅓ cups sugar
grated rind of 1 lemon
1 stick cinnamon
juice of 1 lemon or
    2 tbsps rosewater*

*butter for the pan
flour for rolling out
pistachios for decorating*

1. Butter a 12-inch spring-form pan or an oblong pie pan.
2. For the dough, mix the flour, oil, salt, egg, and luke-warm water, and work into a firm pasta-type dough. With lightly-oiled hands, knead until it is smooth and shiny. Leave to rest for about 30 minutes.
3. For the filling, roughly chop the walnuts, almonds, and pistachios and mix with the sugar.
4. Halve the pastry dough and shape about 16 balls from each half (32 altogether). Flour a pastry board and roll out each ball to a very thin sheet the size of the springform pan, laying them out on a floured tablecloth.
5. Pre-heat the oven to 400°F.

6. Melt the butter without letting it brown.
7. Put a sheet of dough into the springform pan, brush with the melted butter and lay the next sheet on top, brush this with butter and

> ## TIP
>
> *Dough for baklava, known as phyllo dough, can also be bought frozen from supermarkets and middle eastern food stores. To fit it into a springform or rectangular cake pan, it must be buttered and folded several times.*

take the next sheet, and so on, until 10 sheets are in the pan. Spread with half the nut mixture and add another 10 buttered sheets. Add the rest of the nut mixture and the remaining buttered sheets. Finally, pour any remaining butter over the pastry.
8. Use a sharp knife to cut the top layer into diamonds or squares, then bake on the middle shelf of the oven for 50–60 minutes or until golden-brown. Cover with aluminum foil if the pastry looks like browning too quickly.
9. Meanwhile, for the syrup, bring the water, sugar, lemon rind, and cinnamon to the boil, and simmer for 8–10 minutes, then stir in the lemon juice or rosewater. Allow to cool a little, then pour this over the finished pastry. Decorate with pistachios.

Baklava should not be eaten until the next day so that it can totally absorb the syrup.

After the tenth sheet of dough, spread on half the nut filling.

Cut the surface of the pastry with a sharp knife.

Flavor the sugar syrup with lemon and cinnamon, and pour the syrup over the pastry.

ARABIAN ALMOND VOL-AU-VENTS

Sanbusak bil loz
Photo on page 43

MAKES 30 ■
*Preparation and cooking
time: 1 hour
Kcal per portion: 215
P = 4g, F = 13g, C = 32g*

PASTRY:
*½ cup oil
⅔ cup butter
½ cup warm water
1 tsp sugar
4 cups all-purpose flour
flour for rolling out
1 egg for brushing*

FILLING:
*1 cup ground almonds
1 cup sugar
3 tbsps orange-flower water*

1. Line a baking sheet with nonstick baking parchment.
2. For the pastry, warm the oil and butter in a bowl over boiling water until the butter has melted. Mix with the warm water and sugar and put into a large basin.
3. Slowly add the flour, stir-ring constantly, until a soft dough is obtained.
4. For the filling, mix the almonds with sugar and orange-flower water.
5. Pre-heat the oven to 350°F.
6. Roll out the dough thinly on a floured board and use a glass or cookie cutter to cut out 30 rings of about 3 inch-es in diameter. Place 1 tea-spoonful of filling in the middle of each, fold in half into half-moon shapes and press the edges firmly together.
7. Gently beat the egg and brush the tops of the vol-au-vents with it. Arrange on the baking sheet and bake on the middle shelf of the oven for about 30 minutes.

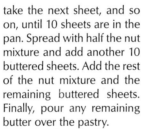

Recipes for Special Occasions

When entertaining discriminating guests for afternoon tea or an important coffee morning, a hostess requires cakes, pastries, and cookies that will impress and delight even the most sophisticated gourmets. Connoisseurs can enjoy Chocolate Mocha Cake, Apricot Flan with Marsala, or Parisian Ring with Raspberry Cream Cheese.

Sophisticated recipes are presented so persuasively in this chapter that even beginners in the art of fine baking will attempt these delicious morsels with success. Useful tips provide ambitious amateur cooks with additional advice on handling sweet fillings.

Filled Jalousies
(see recipe on page 69)

55

ST LUCIA CHERRY CHEESECAKE

SERVES 12 ■ ■ ■
*Preparation and cooking
time: 1 hour 35 minutes
Kcal per portion: 370
P = 12g, F = 19g, C = 39g*

PASTRY:
*⅓ sugar
½ tsp grated lemon rind
3 egg yolks
2 tbsps all-purpose flour
2 tbsps cornstarch
½ tsp baking powder
2 tbsps melted butter
3 egg whites, whisked stiffly
butter for the pan*

FILLING:
*1 package powdered gelatin
3 egg yolks
½ cup sugar
2½ cups cream cheese
1 tsp grated lemon rind
2 tbsps lemon juice
14 ounce can cherries
4 ounces frozen puff dough
4 tbsps raspberry jam
4 tbsps confectioner's sugar
⅔ cup whipped cream*

1. Beat the sugar, lemon rind, and egg yolks into a pale cream. Sift the flour, baking powder, and cornstarch and stir gently into the egg mixture. Stir in the melted butter, a teaspoonful at a time.
2. Fold the stiff egg whites gently into the dough. Put into a buttered 10-inch springform pan and bake on the middle shelf of the oven at 350° for 10–15 minutes.
3. For the filling, soften the gelatin in 2 tbsps cold water. Cream the egg yolks with the sugar. Add the cream cheese, the lemon rind, and 2 tbsps lemon juice. Dissolve the gelatine in 2 tbsps hot water and add it to the mixture. Mix well and leave in a cool place for 15 minutes.
4. Remove the cooled sponge base from the pan and put it on a cake board.

Cut the pastry lid in slices then cover the cheesecake with them.

Cover the springform ring with plastic wrap and put it back round the sponge base. Put in just half the cream cheese mixture. Drain the cherries and reserve 12 for decoration. Arrange the others over the cream cheese layer and cover with the rest of the cream cheese. Leave the cheesecake in a cool place for 2–3 hours.
5. For the lid, roll out the thawed puff dough very thinly, wipe the springform rim clean, and cut out the dough so that it overlaps the rim by ¾ inch all round. Prick the dough all over with a fork and leave in the refrigerator for 15 minutes. Bake on the middle shelf of the oven at 425°F for 10–12 minutes. When cool, spread with jam. Mix the remaining lemon juice with confectioners sugar to make a glaze and spread it over the lid.
6. Before laying the lid on the cheesecake, cut it into 12 slices. Remove the ring from the cheesecake, lay the slices of pastry together on top, and garnish with whipped cream rosettes and the reserved cherries.

APRICOT FLAN WITH MARSALA

SERVES 12 ■ ■ ■
*Preparation and cooking
time: 1 hour 35 minutes
Kcal per portion: 270
P = 6g, F = 11g, C = 32g*

SPONGE:
*½ cup sugar
3 egg yolks
4 tbsps melted butter
1¼ cups all-purpose flour
1 tsp baking powder
3 egg whites
butter for the pan*

FILLING:
*1 tbsp powdered gelatin
12 apricot slices
5 tbsps lemon juice
2 tbsps sugar
2 egg yolks
6 tbsps Marsala
2 egg whites
½ cup cream
1 tsp grated lemon rind
10 peeled apricot halves
3 tbsps apricot jam, sieved
1 tbsp toasted split almonds*

1. For the sponge, beat the sugar and egg yolk until frothy. Stir in the butter. Sift the flour and baking powder, whisk the egg white and add

For this flan it is best to use fresh, ripe apricots.

> ### TIP
> *The apricots are easier to peel if they are first plunged into hot water for a moment. Canned, halved apricots may be used instead.*

these alternately to the egg mixture.
2. Butter a 9-inch springform pan. Put the sponge mixture in it and bake at 350°F on the middle shelf of the oven for 50 minutes. Halfway through the baking time cover with aluminum foil, then finish baking. Loosen the cooked sponge from the pan and leave to cool.
3. Soak the gelatin in 2 tbsps cold water. Pour the lemon juice over the apricot slices.
4. Beat the sugar and egg yolks until pale and creamy. Warm the Marsala and dissolve the gelatin in it. Stir it into the creamed egg yolk and leave in a cool place for 10 minutes. Whisk the egg whites and combine with the yolk mixture, together with the whipped cream, the apricot slices, the lemon juice, and grated lemon rind.
5. Place the cooled sponge on a cake board and replace the springform ring. Cover with the apricot cream and leave in a cold place for 3 hours.
6. Garnish the flan with the apricot halves, round side upward, brush with warmed apricot jam, and sprinkle with the split almonds.

ORANGE LAYER CAKE

SERVES 12 ■ ■ ■
*Preparation and cooking
time: 1 hour 15-25 minutes
Kcal per portion: 495
P = 11g, F = 29g, C = 45g*

SPONGE:
*5 eggs
¾ cup sugar
pinch of salt
6 tbsps all-purpose flour
6 tbsps cornstarch
1 tsp grated lemon rind
4 tbsps melted butter
flour and butter for the pan*

FILLING:
*4 egg yolks
½ cup sugar
2 cups milk
1 vanilla bean
pinch of salt
2 tbsps powdered gelatin
2 cups heavy cream*

FLAVORING:
*juice of 2 oranges
4 tbsps orange liqueur*

DECORATION:
*½ cup toasted split almonds
12 chocolate decorations*

1. For the sponge, beat the eggs, sugar, and salt into a pale yellow cream. Sift the flour and cornstarch and fold in. Add the lemon rind and melted butter.
2. Butter a 9-inch springform pan and dust with flour. Pre-heat the oven to 400°F. Put the sponge mixture into the pan and bake on the middle shelf of the oven for 10 minutes, then lower the heat to 350°F and bake for a further 20 minutes. Test with a wooden skewer and if it comes out sticky, bake for another 5–10 minutes. Remove the sponge from the pan and leave to cool.
3. For the filling, beat the egg yolks and sugar until frothy.
4. Boil the milk with the split vanilla pod and a pinch of salt and pour it gradually into the egg yolk mixture, stirring

Decorate the edge of the sponge with almonds.

vigorously. Remove the vanilla pod. Heat the mixture, beating constantly, until thick enough to stay hanging in drops on the hand whisk. Do not let it boil, or the egg will separate.
5. Dissolve the gelatin in the hot milk and leave to cool. Before the mixture solidifies, whip the cream and fold it in.
6. With the longest knife you have, slice the sponge into 2 or 3 equal layers. Lay the bottom one on a cake board. Mix the orange juice with the orange liqueur and sprinkle one half, or a third, of it over the sponge base.
7. Spread the filling about ½ inch thick on the sponge base. Then add the second (and third) layer and repeat the process. Finally spread the remaining cream round the cake. Leave to set in the refrigerator for 2–3 hours.
8. Stick the almonds by hand round the sides of the cake and decorate the top with the chocolate decorations.

REDCURRANT CHEESECAKE

SERVES 12 ■ ■
*Preparation and cooking
time: 30 minutes
Cooling time: 4 hours
Kcal per portion: 270
P = 13g, F = 12g, C = 27g*

*1 cup graham cracker
  crumbs
2 tbsps ground walnuts
4 tbsps redcurrant jam
1 tsp butter
2 cups redcurrants
2 tbsps powdered gelatin
4 egg yolks
⅔ cup sugar
3 cups cream cheese
6 tbsps lemon or orange juice
4 egg whites
1 tsp salt*

1. Mix the cracker crumbs with the nuts and jam.
2. Butter the ring of an 8-inch springform pan and place it on a cake board. Sprinkle

> **T I P**
>
> *Blueberries can
> be used instead
> of redcurrants,
> which may be
> hard to find.*

the crumb-and-nut mixture evenly inside it.
3. Briefly heat 1 cup redcurrants with 2 tbsps water and then rub through a sieve.
4. Beat the egg yolk and sugar until light and fluffy. Combine the cream cheese, lemon juice, and ½ tsp salt and add to the egg mixture.
5. Dissolve the powdered gelatin in the hot redcurrant juice. Add to the cream cheese mixture.
6. Beat the egg white with the remaining salt until stiff and fold into the cooling mixture. Add the rest of the redcurrants to the cream cheese mixture. Pour the filling over the base. Leave to

Put the crackers in a bag and crush them with a rolling pin.

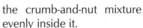

Mix the cracker crumbs with the walnuts and jam.

Put the crumb-and-nut mixture in a buttered cake ring to form the cheesecake base.

set in the refrigerator for about 4 hours.
7. Remove the cake ring and serve the cheesecake cold.

GLAZED PLUM
FLAN

GLAZED PLUM FLAN

SERVES 12 ■ ■

*Preparation and cooking
time: 1 hour 15 minutes
Resting time: 1 hour
Kcal per portion: 295
P = 6g, F = 14g, C = 35g*

PASTRY:

*2 cups all-purpose flour
2 tbsps sugar
pinch of salt
½ tsp lemon rind
1 egg
½ cup butter
butter for the pan*

FILLING AND GLAZE:

*4 eggs
½ cup milk
¼ cup cream
¼ tsp vanilla extract
5 tbsps sugar
2 tbsps plum brandy
    (optional)
3½ cups halved and pitted
    plums*

butter for the pan

*Add the halved plums only when
the glaze begins to thicken.*

Brush the cooked flan with syrup.

1. Sift the flour into a large bowl. Make a well in the middle and put in the sugar, salt, lemon rind, and beaten egg. Mix well together. Flake the chilled butter, scatter it on top and knead quickly to a firm dough. Leave to rest in a cool place for 1 hour.
2. Pre-heat the oven to 425°F.
3. Beat the eggs, milk, cream, vanilla, 3 tbsps sugar, and 1 tbsp plum brandy.
4. Butter a 12-inch springform pan. Roll the dough out to ⅛ inch thick and line the pan with it. Pull up a rim of about 1 inch in height and decorate with a fork. Prick the pastry base all over with a fork and spread the milk mixture over it.
5. Bake on the middle shelf of a preheated oven at 425°F for 15 minutes. As soon as the glaze begins to thicken, take the flan out of the oven and arrange the plums as follows: first lay a circle of halved plums with

their cut side up, then place another half plum cut-side down across every gap. Continue inwards in this way until the flan base is completely covered. Bake for a further 30 minutes, covering the edge with aluminum foil if necessary.
6. Thicken the rest of the plum brandy and sugar in a small pan until a smooth syrup is obtained.
7. After baking, remove the flan from the pan and set it on a rack. Pour the lukewarm syrup over the top and serve lukewarm or cold.

COVERED PEAR FLAN

SERVES 12 ■ ■

*Preparation and cooking
time: 1 hour 15 minutes
Kcal per portion: 295
P = 4g, F = 17g, C = 29g*

*2½ cups all-purpose flour
¾ cup butter
½ tsp salt
⅔ cup water
about 2 pounds pears (may
    be canned)
3 tbsps sugar
3 tbsps lemon juice
freshly ground black pepper
4 tbsps pear brandy liqueur
butter for the pan
1 egg white
1 egg yolk
⅔ cup heavy cream*

1. For the pastry, sift the flour onto a pastry board and flake ⅔ cup chilled butter over it. Rub together to the consistency of fine crumbs. Dissolve the salt in the water and add in small doses, working it in rapidly until a dough is formed. The exact quantity of water will depend on the quality of the flour. Do not knead the dough as this will make it tough. Leave to rest in a cool place for at least 2–3 hours.
2. Peel, quarter, and core the pears. Melt 1 tbsp butter, add the sugar and lightly caramelize. Dilute with the lemon juice and 2 tablespoons of water. Add the prepared pears, grind a dash of pepper over them, and stew for 5–10 minutes or until half-cooked. Take the pears out of the liquid, add the liqueur to it, and reduce over a strong heat to about 3 tablespoons. Pre-heat the oven to 400°F.
3. Butter an ovenproof dish. Roll out two-thirds of the dough to about ⅒ inch thick. Line the dish with it, making a rim of about 1 inch high. Arrange the drained pears in a ring on the dough and

*Arrange the pears in a ring on the
pastry base in the ovenproof dish.*

*Cover the pears with a round
pastry lid and lightly press the
edges of the pastry together.*

bend the rim slightly inward over them. Brush the rim with lightly beaten egg yolk.
4. From the remaining dough cut out a lid the size of the dish. Make a steam hole in the center. Put the lid in place and brush with egg yolk. Decorate with pastry shapes. Brush again with egg yolk.
5. Bake at 425°F on the middle shelf of the oven for about 45 minutes or until golden. If necessary, cover the pie with aluminum foil toward the end of the baking time. Fifteen minutes before the end of cooking, mix the cream with the reduced juice. Using a funnel, pour it into the filling through the steam hole. Serve warm or lukewarm.

PARISIAN RING WITH RASPBERRY CREAM CHEESE

SERVES 12 ■ ■ ■
*Preparation and cooking
time: 1 hour 5 minutes
Kcal per portion: 175
P = 4g, F = 9g, C = 19g*

DOUGH:
*1 cup water
pinch of salt
½ tsp grated orange rind
4 tbsps butter
1¼ cups all-purpose flour
2 eggs
butter for the pan*

FILLING:
*½ cup cream
½ cup cream cheese
2 tbsps sugar
1½ cups raspberries (fresh or
    deep frozen)
1 tbsp Grand Marnier
    (orange liqueur)
1 tbsp confectioner's sugar*

1. Bring the water, salt, sugar, orange rind, and butter to the boil. Remove the pan from the heat and add the sifted flour all at once. Stir with a wooden spoon. Return the pan to the heat and continue to stir over a low flame until the dough comes away from the sides and bottom of the pan (about 3 minutes.) Remove from the heat and work the eggs thoroughly into the dough, one at a time.
2. Butter a 9-inch springform pan and stand it on a baking sheet. Put the dough into a piping bag with a plain nozzle and pipe a 2-inch-wide ring onto the cake pan. Leave in a cool place for 15 minutes.
3. Pre-heat the oven to 350°F, put the ring on the baking sheet on the middle shelf, and bake for 35 minutes. Leave to cool for 2 or 3 minutes then loosen the ring from the sheet and place it on a cake rack.

To produce an accurate ring shape, a border can be drawn on parchment paper. Pipe the dough from a piping bag between the drawn lines.

When the ring is cool, slice it in half horizontally.

Fill the bottom half of the ring with raspberry cream cheese then add the top half as a lid.

4. Whip the cream until stiff, mix with the cream cheese and sugar, and blend in the raspberries and the Grand Marnier. After the ring has cooled, cut it across and fill with the mixture. Dust with confectioner's sugar and set on a cake plate.

FLORENTINES

MAKES ABOUT 25 ■ ■ ■
*Preparation and cooking
time: 50 minutes
Kcal per portion: 155
P = 2g, F = 10g, C = 15g*

*½ cup candied fruits
⅔ cup heavy cream
4 tbsps butter
½ cup chopped split almonds
½ cup sugar
pinch of vanilla sugar
salt
4 tbsps all-purpose flour
½ cup flaked almonds*

GLAZE:
*4 ounces baking chocolate
1 tbsp butter
4 tbsps confectioner's sugar*

1. Chop the candied fruits. Line a baking sheet with nonstick baking parchment.
2. Heat the cream, add the butter, remove the pan from the heat, and put all the ingredients except the almonds into the hot cream. Bring to the boil once more, stirring all the time.
3. Place small mounds of dough well apart on the baking sheet. Arrange the almonds on top and bake at 350°F on the middle shelf of the oven for 20 minutes.
4. As soon as the cookies are firm and golden, take them out of the oven, and use a spatula to loosen them from the paper and turn them over onto a cake rack.
5. For the glaze, melt the chocolate and the butter in a bain-marie, and stir until smooth. Mix in the confectioner's sugar and 2 tablespoons hot water to form a thick chocolate glaze. Thin, if necessary, with another tablespoon of hot water. Coat the Florentines with the glaze, being careful that it stays nice and warm while you are working.

CHOCOLATE FLAN WITH AMARETTI

SERVES 12 ■
*Preparation and cooking
time: 1 hour 5 minutes
Kcal per portion: 235
P = 4g, F = 13g, C = 24g*

*8 ounces frozen puff dough
10 amaretti (small almond
    cookies)
2 tbsps rum
3 eggs
3 tbsps sugar
2 tsps vanilla sugar
1 cup milk
4 ounces baking chocolate*

DECORATION:
1–2 tbsps confectioner's sugar

1. Line a 10-inch springform pan with nonstick baking parchment.
2. Thaw the dough and roll it out, line the pan, and draw up a rim about 2 inches high. Prick the pastry base all over with a fork. Leave in a cool place.
3. Pre-heat the oven to 400°F.
4. Lay the amaretti close together all over the pastry base and moisten with the rum.
5. Whisk the eggs with the sugar and vanilla sugar. Heat the milk and mix with the egg cream, stirring all the time.
6. Break the chocolate into small pieces and sprinkle them over the amaretti. Pour the egg and milk on top and bake on the bottom shelf of the oven for 40 minutes. After 15 minutes, cover with aluminum foil to prevent the flan getting too dark. Lift out onto a cake rack, remove the rim of the springform, and leave the flan to cool.
7. Cut a decorative or appropriate shape out of paper (an Easter bunny for instance), lay it on the flan as a stencil, and dust with the confectioner's sugar.

SWEET YEASTED RASPBERRY CAKE

(Cover photograph)

SERVES 12 ■ ■

Preparation and cooking time: 40 minutes
Rising time for the dough: 1-2 hours
Kcal per portion: 295
P = 4g, F = 15g, C = 25g

DOUGH:
1 tbsp yeast
4 tbsps lukewarm water
2 tbsps sugar
2 cups all-purpose flour
¼ tsp salt
1 tbsp grated lemon rind
2 tbsps butter, diced
1 egg

TOPPING:
butter for the pan
1 tbsp milk
3 tbsps sugar
4 tbsps flaked butter
4 cups raspberries
1 cup sour cream

Pull up a rim and brush it with milk.

Sprinkle 3 tablespoons sugar over the dough base.

Dot butter lumps over the sugar before baking.

1. Cream the yeast with 2 tablespoons water, a pinch of sugar, and 2 tablespoons of flour, and leave to double in bulk.
2. Sift the remaining flour with the salt into a bowl. Make a well in the middle and put in the starter dough, lemon rind, remaining sugar, butter cubes, and egg. Add the rest of the water and knead to a workable firm dough. Shape into a ball, place it in a warmed, floured basin, cover with a cloth, and leave to rise in a warm place for 1 or 2 hours.
3. Pre-heat the oven to 450°F.
4. Roll out the dough into a circle 13 inches across to fit a springform pan. Butter the pan, place the dough on it, and make a rim about ½ inch high.
5. Leave the dough to rise in the pan for another 10 minutes. Brush the rim with milk. Scatter the sugar and butter lumps over the dough base. Bake on the middle shelf of the oven. The surface should only be lightly browned; if necessary protect it with aluminum foil.
6. Serve lukewarm or cold, with raspberries and sour cream. Put some raspberries on each slice and spoon the cream over them.

SPICY YEASTED FRUIT CAKE

SERVES 12–15 ■
Preparation and cooking time: 1 hour
Kcal per portion (15 portions): 380
P = 4g, F = 15g, C = 38g

FILLING:
1 cup dried pears
1 cup dried pitted prunes
½ cup shelled walnuts
pinch of ground cinnamon
pinch of powdered cloves
1 tbsp lemon juice
2 tbsps sugar

DOUGH:
2 cups all-purpose flour
pinch of salt
2 tbsps sugar
½ cup clarified butter
1 egg
1 tbsp cream
1 tsp grated lemon rind
butter for the pan
flour for rolling out

GLAZE:
1 cup heavy cream
3 tbsps honey or pear juice

Soak the dried pears and prunes.

Spread the dried fruit mixture over the pastry.

Pour the sweetened cream over the layer of fruit.

1. For the filling, soak the pears and prunes overnight in cold water at room temperature.
2. For the dough, put the flour, pinch of salt, sugar, and clarified butter into a bowl and rub in to the consistency of fine breadcrumbs. Mix the egg, cream, and lemon rind and add to the mixture. Work all the ingredients rapidly into a dough. Leave to rest at room temperature for 1 hour.
3. Meanwhile, drain the soaked dried fruit and grind it in a food processor. Chop the walnuts coarsely. Mix the fruit, nuts, cinnamon, cloves, lemon rind, and sugar together.
4. Butter a baking sheet. Roll the dough out on a floured pastry board and lay it on the baking sheet. Raise the edges a little. Spread it evenly with the fruit mixture.
5. For the glaze, beat the honey or thickened juice into the cream and pour this over the fruit filling. Bake the cake on the middle shelf of the oven at 430°F for about 30–35 minutes. Leave to cool then cut into fingers.

CHOCOLATE AND WALNUT SQUARES

MAKES ABOUT 50 ■ ■ ■
*Preparation and cooking
time: 2 hours 20 minutes
Kcal per square: 170
P = 2g, F = 10g, C = 18g*

14 ounces (14 squares)
    baking chocolate
4 tbsps water
4 eggs
1⅓ cups brown sugar
6 tbsps butter
1 cup all-purpose flour
¾ cup ground walnuts
1 tbsp butter for the pan

FROSTING:
5 ounces baking chocolate
4 tbsps water
1¼ cups confectioner's sugar,
    sifted
1 tbsp butter
⅔ cup halved walnuts for
    decoration

*Cut up the cooked sponge while
still on the baking sheet.*

*Lay the sponge squares on a cake
rack and top with chocolate
frosting.*

*The walnut halves will stick well if
applied to the moist chocolate.*

1. Break the chocolate into small pieces, put in a small container with the water, and melt in a bain marie. Keep warm over a low heat but do not allow to boil.
2. Beat the eggs and sugar until pale and creamy. Melt the butter in the warm chocolate and stir into the

> ### TIP
> *These chocolate dice can be regarded as storage items, since they can be deep-frozen in plastic bags and thawed out in only 25–30 minutes at room temperature.*

egg mixture. Sift the flour into the mixture and fold in with the nuts.
3. Pre-heat the oven to 350°F. Butter a jellyroll pan,

fill it with the mixture so it is about 1 inch thick, and bake on the middle shelf of the oven for about 15 minutes.
4. For the frosting, melt the chocolate and water in a bain marie, add the sifted confectioner's sugar and the butter, and mix well.
5. Remove the sponge from the oven, allow to cool a little, then take a sharp knife and cut it, still warm, into 2-inch squares.
6. Top the sponge squares with frosting and decorate each one with a walnut half.

CHOCOLATE MOCHA CAKE

MAKES 20-25 SLICES ■
*Preparation and cooking
time: 1 hour 30-40 minutes
Kcal per portion (25 slices):
380
P = 3g, F = 12g, C = 64g*

½ cup sugar
pinch of salt
4 eggs
4 tbsps butter
1 cup all-purpose flour
small pinch of baking
    powder
butter for the pan
1 cup strong coffee
2 tbsps rum

FILLING:
1 cup heavy cream
8 ounces baking chocolate
1 tbsp grated orange rind

FROSTING:
4 ounces baking chocolate
4 tbsps strong coffee
1 cup confectioner's sugar,
    sifted
1 tbsp butter
2 tbsps coarsely-chopped
    pistachios

1. Make the sponge the day before. Beat the sugar, salt, and eggs until pale and creamy. Warm the butter and add it lukewarm. Sift the

> ### TIP
> *A store-bought, ready-made sponge can be used. The chocolate cream must be used immediately because it soon sets and becomes impossible to spread.*

flour and baking powder and stir into the mixture. Butter a 10-inch loaf pan, fill with the mixture, and bake at 350°F on the middle shelf of the

*Pour the chocolate mocha
coating over the finished cake
and garnish with coarsely-
chopped pistachios.*

oven for about 40–50 minutes. Turn out onto a cake rack and allow to cool.
2. Mix the warm coffee with the rum and leave to cool.
3. For the filling, put the cream and the broken chocolate into a small pan and heat slowly, stirring well to ensure that the chocolate melts but does not stick. The moment it reaches boiling point, remove it from the heat, add the orange rind, and leave to cool, stirring occasionally.
4. When cool, put the mixture into a food processor, and mix for a few minutes at high speed, when it will become paler and double in volume.
5. Wash and dry the loaf pan. Cut the sponge across into very thin slices. Lay one in the bottom of the pan, moisten it with coffee, and spread with chocolate cream. Continue until the pan is full. The cake is best left in the refrigerator for 24 hours.
6. Unmold the cake and lay it on a sheet of foil.
7. To make the frosting, melt the chocolate with the coffee in a bain marie. Add the sifted confectioner's sugar and add the butter. Mix well and pour this over the cake. Decorate with the pistachios.

WALNUT SANDWICH
COOKIES

WALNUT SANDWICH COOKIES

MAKES 30 ■
*Preparation and cooking
time: 55 minutes
Resting time: 1 hour
Kcal per cookie: 150
P = 2g, F = 10g, C = 13g*

COOKIE DOUGH:
*⅔ cup butter
3 tbsps sugar
1 egg
6 tbsps ground walnuts
2 cups all-purpose flour
pinch of salt*

COATING:
*4 tbsps butter
2 tbsps sugar
2 tbsps ground walnuts
3 tbsps apricot jam
1 tbsp rum
6 tbsps walnut halves*

1. Knead the butter, sugar, beaten egg, ground walnuts, flour, and salt quickly into a

> **TIP**
>
> *Alternatively, these cookies can be made with whole-wheat or spelt flour.*

firm dough. Leave to rest in a cool place for 1 hour.
2. Warm the butter and mix with the sugar, ground walnuts, jam, and rum.
3. Roll out the dough as thinly as possible. Cut out 2-inch rounds and bake at 350°F on the middle shelf of the oven for 15 minutes. Leave to cool on a rack.
4. Spread the coating over half the cookies, and stick them together in pairs. Top with more coating and stick the walnuts on top. Leave to dry on a rack and store in an airtight container.

PIPED COOKIES WITH CHOCOLATE TIPS

MAKES ABOUT 20 ■■
*Preparation and cooking
time: 45 minutes
Kcal per cookie: 135
P = 1g, F = 6g, C = 18g*

COOKIE DOUGH:
*½ cup butter
½ cup sugar
1 egg
1 cup all-purpose flour
1 cup cornstarch
2 tbsps milk
2 tbsps blanched ground
  almonds
4 tbsps apricot jam*

COATING:
*2 ounces chocolate
knob of unsalted butter*

1. Cream the butter. Add the sugar and beaten egg. Sift the flour and cornstarch together and stir in with the milk, a spoonful at a time. Mix in the almonds. Leave to rest in a cool place for 1 hour.
2. Put the dough in a piping bag with a large rose nozzle. Butter a baking sheet or line it with nonstick baking parchment. Pipe horseshoe shapes of cookie dough onto it, leaving plenty of room as they swell when cooking. Set the oven at

> **TIP**
>
> *Almonds are easy to skin if blanched in boiling water. Then when pinched they will just pop out.*

340°F and bake on the middle shelf for about 15 minutes until pale golden. Loosen them from the baking sheet and leave to

Use jam to stick the cookies together in pairs.

Dip the tips of the cookies into melted chocolate.

Allow the chocolate to dry thoroughly or the cookies will stick together.

cool on a rack.
3. Spread jam on half of the cookies and stick them together in pairs. Leave on a board to dry a little.
4. Break up the chocolate, add 1 tablespoon water, and melt in a bain marie.
5. Add the butter; let it melt in the warm chocolate and beat well.
6. Brush the cookie tips with chocolate glaze or dip them in the bowl. Leave to dry on foil.

FILLED JALOUSIES

(Photo on page 54/55)

MAKES 15 ■
*Preparation and cooking
time: 45-50 minutes
Kcal each one: 150
P = 2g, F = 8g, C = 18g*

*6 tbsps raspberry jam
½ tsp ground cinnamon
¼ tsp powdered cloves
1¼ pounds frozen puff dough
2 tbsps sugar*

1. Thoroughly combine the jam and spices. Pre-heat the oven to 350°F.
2. Thaw the dough, roll out to a rectangle ⅛ inch thick and 12 inches long. Fold in half. Next fold the upper half under by a third, then over by a third. Turn the dough over and fold back the unfolded piece like the first half into a "concertina." Using a sharp knife, cut into slices ¼ inch thick.
3. Line a baking sheet with nonstick baking parchment. Arrange the slices at least 1 inch apart, sprinkle with sugar, and bake on the middle shelf of the oven for about 15–20 minutes until golden-brown.
4. Loosen the cookies from the baking sheet, and leave to cool on a cake rack.
5. Spread half the cookies thickly with jam. Lay the other half of the cookies crossways on top, sugar-side downward.

Wholefood Recipes

*I*n wholefood cooking, refined sugar is, of course, totally avoided and snow-white, bleached refined flour is banned from all mixing bowls. Instead fructose, honey, or maple syrup are used as sweeteners and the various mixtures and toppings are enhanced with grains, seeds, almonds, and other nuts, and all kinds of dried fruits. The results are culinary gems that really contain what their tantalising names promise: Mango and Mascarpone Gâteau, Kumquat and Hazelnut Cakes, and Hazelnut and Nougat Cake. The best whole-wheat flour is freshly milled to preserve the nutrients. If you use a home flour-mill to grind your own grains you will be able to taste the difference.

Buckwheat Gâteau with
Blackberry Filling
(see recipe on page 76)

ORANGE AND PISTACHIO SPONGE

SERVES 12 ■■
*Preparation and cooking
time: 2 hours
Kcal per portion: 450
P = 11g, F = 31g, C = 33g*

SPONGE:
*4 eggs, separated
4 tbsps fructose
juice and rind of 1 orange
⅔ cup fine whole-wheat flour,
sifted
4 tbsps ground almonds*

FILLING:
*2 cups heavy cream
1 tbsp fructose
2 tbsps ground pistachios
3 oranges*

TOPPING:
*7 ounces fresh marzipan
4 tbsps pistachios, finely
ground
4 tbsps Amaretto
confectioner's sugar for
rolling out
2 oranges
1 tbsp orange liqueur
1 cup fructose
½ cup coarsely chopped
pistachios*

1. Pre-heat the oven to 400°F.
2. For the sponge, beat the egg yolks, half the fructose, orange juice, and grated rind until frothy. Mix the whole-wheat flour with the almonds and stir into the mixture 1 tbsp at a time. Whisk the egg whites stiffly with the rest of the sugar and fold evenly into the mixture.
3. Line a 9-inch springform pan with nonstick baking parchment and put the sponge mixture into it. Smooth the top and bake on the middle shelf of the oven for 30–40 minutes until golden-brown. Loosen the sponge base from the pan and leave to cool on a cake rack. Slice horizontally.
4. For the filling, whip the cream stiffly, gradually adding the fructose, and stir

Remove the white parts from the oranges as they taste bitter.

in the pistachios. Peel the oranges, taking care to remove all the white parts. With a sharp knife, skin the individual segments. Spread one sponge layer with two thirds of the pistachio cream, arrange the orange segments on it, and lay the second sponge layer on top.
5. For the topping, knead the marzipan with the ground pistachios and the amaretto, sprinkle your worktop with confectioner's sugar, and roll out to a 9-inch circle. Lay it on the cake.
6. Peel off the orange rind and shred it finely. Blanch in boiling water then plunge into cold. Squeeze the oranges, measure off 3 tbsps of juice, and bring to the boil with the liqueur and the sugar. Leave the orange rind to soak in this for 15 minutes, then drain.
7. Put the remaining pistachio cream into a piping bag with a large star nozzle, and decorate the marzipan top with this cream, the orange rind, and the chopped pistachios.

CARROT CAKE

SERVES 12 ■■■
*Preparation and cooking
time: 1 hour 30 minutes
Kcal per portion: 520
P = 10g, F = 34g, C = 44g*

CAKE:
*2 cups grated carrots
½ cup fructose
juice and rind of 1 lemon
4 eggs
1 egg yolk
1½ cups fine whole-wheat
flour, freshly milled and
sifted
1 cup ground hazelnuts
1 tbsp baking powder
½ cup melted butter
oil for the pan*

TOPPING:
*5 tbsps cream
5 tbsps milk
⅔ cup nougat candy
6 squares milk chocolate
1 cup marzipan
1 cup grated carrots
some carrot tops*

1. Mix the grated carrots for the cake with half the fructose, lemon juice, and grated lemon rind.
2. Pre-heat the oven to 400°F.
3. Put the eggs and egg yolk with the rest of the fructose into a stainless steel bowl and beat to a thick foam in a bain marie. Take out the bowl and continue to beat until cool. Mix the flour with 4oz hazelnuts and the baking powder, and stir into the egg mixture, alternately with the melted butter and the carrots.
4. Oil a 9-inch springform pan and scatter the rest of the hazelnuts in the bottom. Put the mixture in, smooth the top, and bake on the middle shelf of the oven for 20–30 minutes. Release the cake from the pan and leave to cool on a cake rack.
5. For the topping, warm the cream and milk over a low heat and add the crumbled nougat and chocolate, stirring until dissolved. Allow to cool to about 90°F then

Grate the peeled carrots coarsely with a hand-held grater, or a food processor.

Carefully heat the cream, milk, nougat and chocolate, stirring all the time.

spread it evenly over the cake.
6. For the topping, knead the grated carrots into the marzipan, roll the mixture into tiny "carrots", arrange them in a ring on the cake, and decorate with some of their own feathery leaves. Serve with whipped cream.

MANGO AND MASCARPONE GÂTEAU

SERVES 12 ■ ■
*Preparation and cooking
time: 1 hour 30 minutes
Kcal per portion: 500
P = 15g, F = 34g, C = 32g*

CAKE:
*4 ounces plain chocolate
   cake covering
6 eggs, separated
4 tbsps fructose
1¼ cups fine whole-wheat
   flour, freshly milled and
   sifted
6 tbsps melted butter or
   margarine
fat or oil for the pan*

FILLING:
*2 tbsps powdered gelatin
2 medium-sized ripe mangoes
2 cups mascarpone or cream
   cheese
2 tbsps fructose
½ cup heavy cream*

TOPPING:
*1–2 fully ripe, medium-sized
   mangoes
7 tbsps chopped pistachios*

*Whisk the egg whites stiffly with
the fructose and heap on top of
the frothy yolks.*

*Sieve the mango and mascarpone
or purée with a blender.*

1. For the cake, break up the chocolate, melt it in the bain-marie, then leave to cool.
2. Pre-heat the oven to 400°F.
3. Beat the egg yolks and 2 tbsps fructose together until frothy, and add the melted chocolate a little at a time, beating constantly. Whisk the egg whites stiffly with the rest of the fructose and pile on top of the frothy mixture. Sift the flour over this and stir into the mixture with the melted butter. Put in a greased 9-inch springform pan and bake on the middle shelf of the oven for 30–40 minutes. Loosen the cake from the pan and leave to cool on a cake rack, then cut in half horizontally.
4. For the filling, soak the gelatin in cold water. Peel the mangoes, scrape the flesh from the stones, and

purée finely with the mascarpone and fructose. Dissolve powdered gelatin in 3 tbsps hot water and stir carefully into the fruit mixture. As soon as this begins to set, stir in the whipped cream.
5. Spread the lower layer of cake with two thirds of the filling, add the next layer and spread the remaining filling on top.
6. For the decoration, peel the mangoes, cut the flesh from the stone in thin slices, and fan them out over the surface of the cake. Sprinkle the sides and top with the pistachios. Serve well chilled.

LEMON FLAN

SERVES 12 ■ ■
*Preparation and cooking
time: 1 hour
Resting time: 1 hour 30
minutes
Kcal per portion: 210
P = 4g, F = 14g, C = 16g*

DOUGH:
*1 cup fine whole-wheat flour,
   freshly milled and sifted
2 tbsps ground almonds
3 tbsps fructose
1 egg
½ cup chilled butter*

FILLING:
*3 tbsps butter
3 tbsps fructose
2 eggs
juice of 3 lemons
grated rind of 2 lemons
blanched or candied lemon
   or citron slices*

*flour for rolling out
oil for the pan*

1. For the dough, sift the flour onto a pastry board, and mix with the almonds and fructose. Make a well in the middle, break in the egg, and flake the chilled butter round the edge. Chop with a chef's knife, then knead quickly with both hands into a smooth dough. Wrap in foil and refrigerate for 1 hour.
2. Roll out the dough on a floured pastry board to a circle 10 inches across. Grease a 9-inch springform pan, line with the dough and make a rim ½ inch high. Prick

*Stir the buttercream until it
thickens and forms bubbles.*

*For the topping, the slices of
lemon can be blanched or
candied.*

4. Place the pan on the middle shelf of the oven and bake for about 10 minutes until golden. Leave in the pan until it has cooled a little.
5. For the topping, melt the butter in a skillet over a low heat and stir in the other ingredients. Continue stirring until the cream thickens and forms bubbles. Do not beat to a foam.
6. Loosen the pastry base from the pan and fill it with the lemon cream. Serve well chilled. Decorate according to taste with blanched or candied slices of lemon or citron.

> **TIP**
>
> *Alternatively, this
> cake can be made
> with orange juice
> and grated
> orange rind.*

the base all over with a fork. Leave the pan in a cool place for another 30 minutes.
3. Pre-heat the oven to 400°F.

BUCKWHEAT GÂTEAU WITH BLACKBERRY FILLING

Photograph on page 70/71

SERVES 12 ■■
*Preparation and cooking
time: 45 minutes
Kcal per portion: 295
P = 6g, F = 20g, C = 22g*

SPONGE:
*3 eggs, separated
½ cup honey
1 cup buckwheat flour, sifted
1 cup whole-wheat flour,
 sifted*

FILLING:
*4 cups fresh blackberries
2 cups heavy cream
½ cup ground pistachios*

*fat or oil for the pan
3 tbsps buckwheat grits
 (kasha)*

1. Pre-heat the oven to 400°F.
2. Beat the egg yolks and honey until frothy. Mix the two kinds of flour, sift over the egg mixture and stir in. Whisk the egg whites stiffly and fold into the mixture. Grease a 9-inch springform pan, sprinkle it with buckwheat grits, fill with the sponge mixture, and bake on the middle shelf of the oven for about 15 minutes.
3. Loosen the sponge from the pan, leave to cool, then slice in half horizontally.
4. Hull and clean the blackberries. Whip the cream stiffly. Purée 3 cups of blackberries and mix them with the pistachios into the cream. Fill the sponge with half the cream mixture, spread the rest over the top, and garnish with the remaining blackberries. This gâteau is also delicious made with raspberries or blueberries.

RHUBARB TART

SERVES 12 ■■
*Preparation and cooking
time: 1 hour
Kcal per portion: 85
P = 4g, F = 2g, C = 11g*

*1 pound frozen whole-wheat
puff dough*

FILLING:
*1½ pounds rhubarb
1 cup small curd cottage
 cheese
2 eggs, separated
3 tbsps fructose
1 tbsp arrowroot or potato
 starch
juice and rind of 1 lemon
4 tsps rum*

*flour for rolling out
oil for the pan
dried beans for blind baking
2 tbsps apricot jam
4 tsps raspberry liqueur*

1. Thaw the slabs of dough side-by-side, then lay one on top of the other on a floured board and roll out to a circle ¼ inch thick and 12 inches in diameter. Grease a 9-inch pie pan, lay the dough in it, and raise a rim 1 inch high. Leave in a cool place for 20 minutes.
2. Pre-heat the oven to 400°F.
3. For the filling, rinse the rhubarb, skin it only if necessary, and cut into 1-inch pieces.
4. Line the pastry base with nonstick baking parchment, weight it with some dried beans, and bake on the middle shelf of the oven for 10 minutes, then remove the paper and beans.
5. Meanwhile combine the cheese, egg yolks, fructose, and arrowroot and flavor with the lemon juice, grated rind, the pulp of the vanilla bean, and the rum. Whisk the egg whites stiffly and fold evenly into the cheese mixture.
6. Spread the cheese mixture over the baked pastry

Roll out the dough on a board to a thickness of ¼ inch.

Lay the dough in the pan and make a rim 1 inch high.

Lay nonstick baking parchment over the pastry in the pan and weight with dried beans.

case, decorate with the rhubarb, and bake on the middle shelf of the oven for 10–15 minutes.
7. Warm the apricot jam and raspberry liqueur in a small pan over a low heat, and glaze the flan with it, using a pastry brush.

CITRUS LOAF

SERVES 12 ■
*Preparation and cooking
time: 1 hour 30 minutes
Kcal per portion: 370
P = 7g, F = 25g, C = 30g*

*3 oranges
3 lemons
1¼ cups butter or margarine,
 softened
½ cup fructose
6 eggs, separated
2½ cups whole-wheat flour,
 sifted*

oil and flour for the pan

1. Peel 2 oranges and 2 lemons, removing all the white parts. Remove the pulp from the segment skins using a sharp knife. Squeeze the remaining orange and lemon.
2. Pre-heat the oven to 400°F.
3. Cream the softened fat with 6 tbsps fructose. Add the egg yolks, flour, and fruit juice alternately, a little at a time, stirring continuously. Whisk the egg whites stiffly with the remaining fructose and stir evenly into the mixture with the citrus segments.

TIP

The finished cake can be sprinkled with confectioner's sugar or spread with melted apricot jam.

4. Oil and flour a 3-quart loaf pan. Fill with the cake mixture and bake on the middle shelf of the oven for about 1 hour, or until golden-brown.

KUMQUAT AND HAZELNUT CAKES

MAKES 10 ■ ■ ■
Preparation and cooking time: 1 hour 20 minutes
Kcal per cake: 965
P = 16g, F = 63g, C = 80g

BASE:
7 eggs, separated
2 tbsps fructose
1 tsp ground cinnamon
juice and rind of 1 lemon
2½ cups ground filberts (hazelnuts)
1 cup whole-wheat cake or zwieback crumbs

FILLING:
1 cup heavy cream
1 vanilla bean
4 tbsps fructose
1 cup arrowroot or potato starch
3 tbsps orange liqueur
⅓ cup butter
2 tbsps creamed coconut
1 cup kumquats
½ cup white wine

COVERING:
1 cup marzipan
1 tbsp orange liqueur
confectioner's sugar

GLAZE:
5 tbsps milk
5 tbsps cream
1½ cups nut paste
10 squares chocolate

1. Pre-heat the oven to 400°F.
2. For the base, beat the egg yolks, sugar, and cinnamon together until frothy. Gradually add the lemon juice, grated lemon rind, nuts, and cake or zwieback crumbs, beating all the time. Whisk the egg whites until stiff and fold evenly into the mixture. Line two baking sheets with nonstick baking parchment, spread the mixture over them, and bake, one at a time, on the middle shelf of the oven for about 10 minutes.
3. Leave the cakes to cool,

then remove the paper and cut out 10 2½-inch circles. Cut the rest into small pieces and set aside for the filling.
4. For the filling, reserve 3 tbsps of the cream and bring the rest to the boil with the inside of the vanilla bean and 3 tbsps sugar. Stir the arrowroot or potato starch into the reserved cream with 4 tsps orange liqueur and pour into the boiling cream, stirring well. Allow to boil up once, then dissolve the butter and the creamed coconut in it and remove it from the heat.
5. Wash and halve the kumquats, remove any seeds, and slice them thinly. Put the white wine, the rest of the orange liqueur and fructose in a pan, bring to the boil, and simmer the sliced fruit in it for 2–3 minutes. Tip the fruit into a sieve and drain. Reserve 20 slices for decoration, finely chop the rest, and mix with the cooled cream, together with the reserved cake crumbs.
6. Put the filling into a piping bag with a large round nozzle and pipe it over 10 of the bases. Cover these with the other 10.
7. For the covering, mix the liqueur with the marzipan and add enough confectioner's sugar to produce a smooth mixture. Dust a pastry board with confectioner's sugar, roll out the marzipan, cut 10 2½-inch circles, and cover the cakes with them.
8. For the glaze, put the milk and cream into a pan, bring to the boil, add the nut paste and chocolate, and stir until dissolved. Leave to cool to lukewarm.
9. Lay the cakes on a cake rack with a drip-tray underneath and pour the liquid glaze over them. Before it sets, decorate each cake with a couple of kumquat slices.

Cut individual rounds from the baked sheet of cake.

After boiling the kumquat slices in wine and orange liqueur, drain them well.

Cover each of the filled cakes with marzipan.

HAZELNUT AND NOUGAT CAKE

SERVES 12 ■ ■
Preparation and cooking time: 1 hour 15 minutes
Kcal per portion: 480
P = 10g, F = 33g, C = 35

BASE:
½ cup nut paste
8 egg yolks
6 tbsps fructose
2½ cups ground filberts (hazelnuts)
6 egg whites
oil for the pan

TOPPING:
5 tbsps cream
1 cup nut paste
4 ounces baking chocolate
4 ounces milk chocolate caraque or milk chocolate flake

1. For the base, chop the nut paste into small pieces, put them into a metal basin, warm in a bain-marie, and leave to cool.
2. Pre-heat the oven to 400°F.
3. Beat the egg yolks and half the fructose until frothy and add the melted nut paste, beating continuously. Whisk the egg whites into stiff peaks with the rest of the sugar, heap onto the frothy mixture, and scatter the hazelnuts on top. Stir together evenly, put the mixture into a greased 9-inch springform pan, and bake on the middle shelf of the oven for 30–40 minutes.
4. Release the base from the pan and leave to cool.
5. For the topping, bring the cream to the boil, reduce the heat, and dissolve the nougat and baking chocolate in it. Let the mixture cool to lukewarm then coat the cake with it. Sprinkle with chocolate flake or caraque and leave to set.

Quick and Easy Recipes

*E*ven people who always have to do their cooking with one eye on the clock needn't limit themselves to mundane recipes. The following pages contain many ideas for lightning-quick cakes, pastries, and gâteaux that will certainly find favor even with gourmets. Although many of the cake and pastry bases are not homemade, the toppings and fillings are appetizing enough to leave no taste unsatisfied. This collection of quick recipes ranges from Pear Flan with Almond Topping to super-speedy Cream Buns.

Apple Flan
(see recipe on page 82)

TIRAMISÙ

SERVES 12
Preparation time: 10 minutes
Kcal per portion: 270
P = 8g, F = 15g, C = 25g

1 chocolate sponge cake base
   (storebought)
½ cup strong coffee
2 cups mascarpone or cream
   cheese
4 tbsps sugar
1 egg yolk
2 tbsps amaretto liqueur
3 tbsps cocoa powder for
   dusting

*Moisten the sponge base evenly
with the coffee.*

*Whisk the mascarpone, sugar,
and egg yolk until creamy.*

1. Set the sponge base on a
cake board and moisten it
with coffee.
2. Beat the mascarpone or
cream cheese with the sugar
and egg yolk until creamy,
stir in the amaretto, and
spread this over the sponge.
3. Dust the top thickly with
cocoa powder. Tiramisù
tastes particularly good
when well-chilled.

APRICOT CREAM FLAN

SERVES 12
*Preparation and cooking
time: 40 minutes*
Kcal per portion: 160
P = 3g, F = 5g, C = 24g

8 ounces sweet shortcrust
   dough (fresh or chilled)
fat or oil for the pan
2 eggs, separated
2 tbsps sugar
4 tbsps sour cream
1 tbsp rum
2 cups apricot halves
   (canned or bottled)

1. Pre-heat the oven to 350°F.
2. Grease a 10-inch springform pan, line it with sweet
shortcrust dough, raise a 1-
inch rim, prick the base all
over with a fork, and bake on
the middle shelf of the oven
for 15 minutes.
3. Meanwhile, beat the egg
yolks with the sugar until
frothy, and stir in the sour
cream and rum. Whisk the
egg whites stiffly and gently
fold in.
4. Drain the apricots in a
sieve, take the baked pastry
base from the oven, arrange
the apricots on it, and cover
with the cream mixture.
5. Bake for a further 20–25
minutes at the same temperature. Other fruits may be
used instead of apricots.
Decorate the cake with
sprigs of fresh mint or lemon
balm just before serving.

APPLE FLAN

Photograph on page 81

SERVES 12
*Preparation and cooking
time: 40 minutes*
Kcal per portion: 105
P = 1g, F = 5g, C = 11g

8 ounces flaky dough (fresh
   or chilled)
fat or oil for the pan
2 or 3 tart, green apples
juice of ½ lemon
2 tbsps apricot jam

1. Pre-heat the oven to
400°F.
2. Roll out the dough.
Grease a 9-inch springform
pan, line it with the dough
and raise an edge 1 inch
high.
3. Rinse, peel, quarter, and
core the apples, slice them
finely with a slicer, sprinkle
with lemon juice and
arrange them evenly over
the dough.
4. Bake on the middle shelf
of the oven for 25 minutes.
5. Warm the apricot jam and
brush the still-warm flan with
it. Apple flan tastes best
when freshly-baked. Serve
with whipped cream.
Instead of apricot jam, the
apple flan can be sprinkled
with a mixture of sugar and
cinnamon.

PEAR AND ALMOND FLAN

SERVES 12
*Preparation and cooking
time: 40 minutes*
Kcal per portion: 180
P = 4g, F = 10g, C = 19g

3 large, ripe pears
1 cup water
1 tbsp lemon juice
⅔ cup crème fraîche or sour
   cream
3 egg yolks
3 tbsps sugar
3 tbsps ground almonds
1 tsp cinnamon
fat or oil for the pan
10 ounces sweet shortcrust
   pastry (fresh or chilled)

1. Peel and core the pears
and cut them into thin slices.
2. Bring the water to the boil
in a pan with the lemon
juice, and simmer the pear
slices for 2 minutes. Pour off
the liquid and drain the
slices.

> **TIP**
>
> ***This flan tastes
> excellent served
> lukewarm with
> cream.***

3. Pre-heat the oven to
400°F.
4. For the filling, beat together the crème fraîche or sour
cream, egg yolks, sugar,
almonds, and cinnamon.
5. Grease a 10-inch springform pan. Partly roll out the
dough then press by hand
into the pan, raising an edge
1 inch high.
6. Arrange the pear slices
evenly round the dough,
pour the filling over them,
and bake the flan on the middle shelf of the oven for 25
minutes.

HAZELNUT CAKE

SERVES 12 ■
*Preparation and cooking
time: 45 minutes
Kcal per portion: 275
P = 5g, F = 16g, C = 29*

⅔ cup softened butter
⅔ cup sugar
2 eggs
1 pinch of salt
2 cups all-purpose flour
2 tsps baking powder
about 8 tbsps milk
1 cup ground filberts
  (hazelnuts)
2 tbsps cocoa powder
2 tbsps confectioner's sugar

1. Pre-heat the oven to 400°F.
2. Beat the butter until creamy and gradually pour in the sugar. Beat in the eggs, add the pinch of salt, and stir well.
3. Sift together the flour and baking powder, and add to

> ### TIP
> *The cake can be sliced through and filled with cream, but this takes a little longer.*

the mixture alternately with the milk. Lastly add the ground filberts.
4. Grease a 9-inch springform pan, fill with the mixture, smooth the top, and bake on the middle shelf of the oven for 30 minutes.

PEACH SLICE

SERVES 8 ■
*Preparation and cooking
time: 35 minutes
Kcal per portion: 475
P = 12g, F = 24, C = 52*

4 eggs, separated
3–4 tbsps lukewarm water
⅔ cup sugar
2 tbsps vanilla sugar
1¼ cups all-purpose flour
1 pinch baking powder
4 cups (2 pounds) canned
  peach halves
2 cups double cream cheese
½ cup heavy cream
confectioner's sugar for
  dusting

1. Pre-heat the oven to 400°F. Line a jellyroll pan with nonstick baking parchment.
2. Beat the egg yolks to a foam with the water, then add the sugar and half the vanilla sugar. Whisk the egg whites stiffly and pile on top of the creamed egg yolks. Mix the flour and baking powder and sift over the egg white. Fold together carefully with a metal spoon.
3. Spread the sponge mixture over the prepared jellyroll pan and bake on the middle shelf of the oven for 15 minutes or until golden.
4. Drain the peaches in a sieve.
5. Beat the cream cheese in a bowl. Whip the cream until stiff with the rest of the vanilla sugar and stir into the cream cheese.
6. Turn the cooked sponge out at once onto a cake rack and cut in half.
7. Spread half the filling on one layer of sponge, arrange the peaches on top, pressing them in, cover with the rest of the filling, smooth flat, and top with the second sponge. Dust with confectioner's sugar and cut into 8 slices.

Mix the flour and baking powder and sift into the creamed egg yolks.

Spread the sponge mixture over the lined baking sheet.

Turn the cooked sponge out onto a cake rack and cut in half.

Spread one half with cream cheese filling and arrange the peach halves on it.

NUT MERINGUE FLAN

SERVES 12 ■
*Preparation and cooking
time: 40 minutes
Kcal per portion: 345
P = 5g, F = 23g, C =29g*

8 ounces sweet shortcrust
  dough (fresh or chilled)
fat or oil for the pan
2 tbsps apricot jam
½ cup butter
3 tbsps sugar
2 tbsps water
1 cup ground filberts
  (hazelnuts)
1 cup chopped filberts
  (hazelnuts)
2 egg whites

1. Pre-heat the oven to 400°F.
2. Roll out the dough. Grease a 10-inch springform pan and line its base and sides with the dough.
3. Prick the base all over with a fork and brush with the apricot jam.

> ### TIP
> *An accompanying mint-flavored cream tastes refreshing. To make it, cut a bunch of fresh mint into narrow shreds and mix with 1 cup whipped cream.*

4. For the meringue mixture, warm the butter, sugar, and water in a pan and stir until dissolved. Take the pan from the heat and stir in the filberts. Whisk the egg whites until stiff, fold into the mixture, and spread over the base.
5. Bake on the middle shelf of the oven for 25 minutes. Instead of filberts, you can use ground almonds and chopped pecans or butternuts.

RASPBERRY FLAN WITH ALMOND MERINGUE

SERVES 12
Preparation and cooking time: 20 minutes
Kcal per portion: 155
P = 3g, F = 5g, C = 22g

8 ounces sweet shortcrust
    dough
fat or oil for the pan
2 tbsps raspberry jam
1 tbsp rum
2½ cups fresh raspberries
3 egg whites
4 tbsps sugar
2 tbsps ground almonds
confectioner's sugar for
    dusting

1. Pre-heat the oven to 350°F.
2. Grease a 10-inch spring-form pan and line the base and sides with dough. Prick the base all over with a fork and bake on the middle shelf of the oven for 15 minutes.

> **TIP**
>
> *This flan makes a wonderful dinner-party dessert.*

3. Meanwhile, beat the jam and rum together in a small basin.
4. Rinse the raspberries and allow to drain thoroughly.
5. For the meringue, whisk the egg whites and sugar until stiff, and fold in the ground almonds.
6. Brush the cooked pastry with the jam-and-rum mixture, fill with the raspberries, cover with the meringue mixture, dust with confectioner's sugar and bake for a further 5 minutes at 425°F or until golden.

PIG-EARS

MAKES 12
Preparation and cooking time: 25 minutes
Kcal per portion: 190
P = 2g, F = 10g, C = 22g

2 x 8-ounce packages puff
    dough
½ cup sugar

1. Pre-heat the oven to 425°F.
2. Sprinkle the worktop with sugar. Roll out the dough from one package length-wise and sprinkle the top with sugar, then cut into two pieces and lay one on top of the other.
3. Treat the second package in the same way, so you now have a pile of four layers.
4. Carefully roll the dough into a rectangle about 6x14 inches. Mark the center and roll the two ends inward, sprinkle with sugar, and fold together again like a book.
5. Rinse a baking sheet with cold water. Cut the pastry roll into slices ½ inch thick, lay them on the baking sheet, and bend the two lower ends slightly outwards. Leave plenty of room between them.
6. Bake on the middle shelf for about 10 minutes until the undersides brown, then turn them over and give them another 5 minutes to finish cooking. Brown sugar may be used instead of white, or half the sugar may be replaced by ground nuts.

Roll out the flaky pastry on a sugared worktop.

Cut the dough in two and lay the halves one on top of the other.

Roll the two ends of the pastry evenly to the middle.

Cut the rolled-up dough into ½-inch slices and lay them on a wet baking sheet.

POPPYSEED POCKETS

MAKES 16
Preparation and cooking time: 20 minutes
Kcal per portion: 180
P = 4g, F = 11g, C = 17g

2 x 8-ounce packages puff
    dough
flour for rolling out
1 egg, separated
1 cup poppyseed filling
    (storebought)

1. Pre-heat the oven to 400°F.
2. Lightly roll out the puff dough on a floured worktop and cut into 16 equal 3-inch squares. Brush the edges with egg white.
3. Place a teaspoonful of poppyseed filling in the middle of each square and fold it over diagonally. Use your

> **TIP**
>
> *Because these poppyseed pockets are so easy to handle they are ideal for picnics and parties.*

fingers to press the edges together. Paint the top of each triangle with beaten egg yolk.
4. Rinse a baking sheet with cold water, arrange the poppyseed pockets on it and bake on the middle shelf of the oven for 12 minutes. Instead of poppyseed, the pockets can be filled with a mixture of cream cheese and egg, spiced up with rum-soaked raisins.

CREAM BUNS

MAKES 6 ■
*Preparation and cooking
time: 25 minutes
Kcal per portion: 330
P = 4g, F = 23g, C = 26g*

*8 ounces puff dough
flour for rolling out
¾ cup heavy cream
2 tbsps vanilla sugar
3 tbsps amaretto
2 tbsps chopped pistachios
confectioner's sugar for
    dusting*

1. Pre-heat the oven to 400°F.
2. Roll out the pastry on a lightly floured worktop and stamp out 6 rounds 4 inches in diameter.
3. Rinse a baking sheet with cold water, set the dough rounds on it and bake on the

Cut out 4-inch rounds of puff dough.

Add all the other ingredients to the whipped cream.

Cut the buns in half and leave to cool.

TIP

The cream can be mixed with fresh raspberries, strawberries, or blueberries. Sliced bananas also taste very good.

---

middle shelf of the oven for 12 minutes or until golden.
4. Meanwhile, whip the cream until stiff. Add the vanilla sugar and finally the amaretto and pistachios.
5. Take the pastries out of the oven and slice in half. Allow to cool, then fill with amaretto cream. Dust with confectioner's sugar.
If the cream buns are made for a children's birthday party, the amaretto should be replaced by 1 tsp almond extract.

Pile the amaretto cream onto the lower half of each bun and top with a lid.

MARZIPAN CUPCAKES

MAKES 20 ■
*Preparation and cooking
time: 35 minutes
Kcal per portion: 155
P = 3g, F = 7g, C = 20g*

*½ cup butter
½ cup sugar
2 tbsps vanilla sugar
pinch of salt
2 eggs
½ cup marzipan
2 cups all-purpose flour
2 tsps baking powder
3 tbsps milk*

*20 paper cupcake cases
confectioner's sugar for
    dusting*

1. Pre-heat the oven to 350°F.
2. Beat the butter, sugar, vanilla sugar, and salt until creamy. Beat in the eggs.

TIP

You can frost the cakes with confectioner's sugar mixed with cranberry juice, which turns out a strong pink.

---

3. Crumble the marzipan finely, add it to the mixture, and beat until it has melted.
4. Sift the flour with the baking powder and fold in. Stir in the milk and work to a smooth dough which should drop heavily and slowly from the spoon.
5. Put a level tablespoon of dough into each cupcake case, arrange them all on a baking sheet and bake on the middle shelf of the oven for about 20 minutes. Dust with confectioner's sugar and serve with coffee or tea.

PUFF PASTRY SLICES WITH CRANBERRY CREAM

MAKES 10 ■
*Preparation and cooking
time: 20 minutes
Kcal per portion: 325
P = 2g, F = 15g, C = 31g*

*10 ounces frozen puff dough,
    thawed
1 cup heavy cream
4 tbsps confectioner's sugar
3 tbsps canned or frozen
    cranberries
1 tbsp rum
confectioner's sugar for
    dusting*

1. Pre-heat the oven to 400°F.
2. Halve the packages of puff dough, lay them on a baking sheet rinsed in cold water, and bake on the middle shelf of the oven for 12–14 minutes.
3. Meanwhile, for the filling, whip the cream and confectioner's sugar until stiff, then add the cranberries and rum.
4. Take the pastry out of the oven, cut the pieces crosswise, and leave to cool.
5. Heap the cranberry cream on the bottom layer of pastry, cover with the top layer, and serve dusted with confectioner's sugar.

YEASTED WHORLS WITH WALNUT OR PECAN FILLING

MAKES 16
Preparation and cooking time: 20 minutes
Kcal per portion: 130
P=2g, F=6g, C=17g

1 cup walnuts or pecans
12 ounces yeast dough (fresh or chilled)
flour for rolling out
oil for the baking sheet
1 cup confectioner's sugar
4 tbsps lemon juice

1. Finely grind the walnut or pecan nutmeats in a food processor.
2. Pre-heat the oven to 400°F.
3. Roll out the yeast dough into a rectangle on a lightly-floured work top.

The quickest way to grind walnuts is in the food processor.

4. Distribute the ground walnuts evenly over the dough. Firmly roll up the sheet of dough, starting from one of the long sides, and then cut this roll into ¾-inch slices.
5. Lay the yeast whorls on an oiled baking sheet, and bake on the middle shelf for 10–12 minutes, or until golden-brown.
6. For the topping, mix together the lemon juice and confectioner's sugar in a cup, and then brush this over each whorl.

COCONUT TRIANGLES

MAKES 6
Preparation and cooking time: 25 minutes
Kcal per portion: 305
P=11g, F=17g, C=26g

3 tbsps raisins
2 tbsps rum
1 cup small-curd cottage cheese
2 egg yolks
2 tbsps vanilla sugar
3 tbsps shredded coconut
9 ounces puff dough
flour for rolling out
1 egg, separated

1. Pre-heat the oven to 350°F.
2. Put the raisins to soak in the rum.
3. Put the cottage cheese in a bowl. Add the egg yolk, the vanilla sugar, and the shredded coconut, and mix well. Add the soaked raisins.
4. Roll out the puff dough on a floured work top until it is ¼ inch thick. Using a pastry wheel, cut out 6 x 4-inch squares. Place equal amounts of the cheese mixture in the middle of each.
5. Brush the edges of the pastry squares with egg white, fold each over, and press the sides together to make six triangles. Brush the triangles with egg yolk.
6. Rinse a baking sheet with cold water. Place the puff pastry triangles on the sheet, spacing them out well. Bake on the middle shelf for 12 minutes or until golden-brown.

Stir together the cottage cheese, egg yolk, vanilla sugar, shredded coconut, and rum-soaked raisins.

Roll out the puff dough on a floured work top until it is ¼ inch thick.

Cut out little squares with a pastry wheel.

Distribute equal amounts of coconut-and-cottage-cheese filling to each little square of pastry. Brush the edges with egg white, fold over and press together to make into triangles.

BANANA CROISSANTS

MAKES 6
Preparation and cooking time: 20 minutes
Kcal per portion: 195
P=2g, F=10g, C=23g

9 ounces puff dough
flour for rolling out
6 tsps marmalade
1 large or 2 small ripe bananas

1. Pre-heat the oven to 400°F.
2. Roll out the puff dough on a lightly floured work top. Cut the pastry into 6 x 4-inch squares.
3. Spread 1 tsp marmalade on each square.
4. Peel and thinly slice the banana and distribute evenly among the pastry squares.

> **TIP**
>
> *Pitted, diced plums can be substituted for the bananas, and, if desired, these can first be soaked for 10 minutes in a plum-flavored liqueur or in vodka*

5. Starting at one corner, roll each piece up, squeeze the ends together well and bend them into croissant shapes.
6. Rinse a baking sheet with cold water. Lay the banana croissants on the sheet, and bake on the middle shelf for 12–15 minutes.
The croissants taste best when warm, and are good for Sunday brunch.

91

If you want to use the rapid microwave method for baking, you are better off using a combination oven, which has a slightly smaller volume than the conventional oven. It will brown the mixture using the conventional baking heat, while fruit and other ingredients cook quickly and gently under microwave power. Some of the recipes described here for luscious cakes and sumptuous gâteaux enable a time-saving of over 50 per cent. Remember when baking in the microwave to use only suitable containers, which can be bought in all shapes and sizes. Metal cake pans are totally taboo in the microwave.

Wholefood Pear Cake with Walnut Topping (see recipe on page 98)

BADEN APPLE CAKE

SERVES 12 ■■
Combination MW
Preparation and cooking
time: 1 hour
Kcal per portion: 470
P = 7g, F = 31g, C = 41g

8 tart, green apples (e.g.
    Newtown pippin)
juice of 1 lemon
1 cup butter or margarine
1 cup sugar
5 eggs, separated
2 cups all-purpose flour
2 tsps baking powder
4 tbsps chopped walnuts
4 tbsps grated chocolate
fat or oil for the mold

TOPPING:
1 cup heavy cream
4 tbsps flake or caraque
    chocolate
1 small, red apple

Grate the peeled apples coarsely and pour lemon juice over them.

Sprinkle flaked chocolate evenly over the cream coating.

1. Peel the apples, grate coarsely, and sprinkle at once with lemon juice.
2. Pre-heat the oven of a combination model to 400°F.
3. Beat the softened fat and sugar until creamy and gradually add the egg yolks. Combine the flour, baking powder, walnuts, and chocolate. Drain the apple and stir

> ### TIP
> *If you want the cake to keep longer, frost it with chocolate frosting.*

into the creamed mixture, alternately with the flour mixture. Whisk the egg whites stiffly and fold in.
4. Put the cake mixture into a microwave cake pan 10 inches in diameter and bake on the middle shelf of the oven for *22–25 minutes at 180 Watts and 400°F (fan-assisted model 375°F).* Remove from the pan and

leave to cool on a cake rack.
5. Whip the cream until stiff. Coat the cake with two-thirds of it and sprinkle with chocolate flake or caraque. Put the remaining cream in a piping bag and decorate the cake with twelve large rosettes. Rinse, halve, and core the red apple and cut into thin slices. Stick the slices in the cream rosettes.

CHEESECAKE FLAN WITH APRICOTS

SERVES 12 ■■
Combination MW
Preparation and cooking
time: 30 minutes
Kcal per portion: 425
P = 9g, F = 24g, C = 42g

DOUGH:
2½ cups all-purpose flour
1 tsp baking powder
pinch of salt
⅔ cup sugar
1 egg
⅔ cup butter

FILLING:
1¾ cups cream cheese (70%
    fat content)
2 egg yolks
2 tbsps apricot jam
2 tbsps apricot brandy
2 tbsps all-purpose flour
5 cups ripe apricots

fat or oil for the mold
3 tbsps apricot jam
2 tbsps apricot brandy

Chop all the pastry ingredients rapidly with a chef's knife.

Smooth the cream cheese filling and set the apricots close together on top.

1. Sift the flour onto a pastry board with the baking powder, salt, and sugar. Make a well in the middle, break in the egg, and flake the chilled butter round the edge. Chop together with a chef's knife then knead quickly by hand to a smooth dough. Wrap

> ### TIP
> *The cake tastes best when well chilled. If possible, make it the day before and refrigerate overnight.*

in foil and leave in a cool place for 30 minutes.
2. Put the cream cheese in a bowl and beat with the egg yolks, jam, brandy, and flour. Wash, halve, and pit the apricots.

3. Pre-heat the combination oven to 425°F.
4. Roll out the sweet short-crust dough into a circle on a floured pastry board. Grease the base and sides of a microwave cake pan 10 inches across and line it with the dough.
5. Spread the cream cheese filling in the pastry case, smooth the top, and cover with the apricots laid close together, cut side down.
6. Bake on the middle shelf of the oven for *18–20 minutes at 180 Watts and 400°F (fan-assisted model 375°F).*
7. Mix the apricot jam and apricot brandy in a small microwave dish and after the cake is done heat it for *1–2 minutes at 600 Watts.* Brush the cake with the liquid jam and leave to cool in the pan.

CHEESECAKE WITH ALMONDS

SERVES 12 ■ ■
*Combination MW
Preparation and cooking
time: 1 hour
Resting time: 30 minutes
Kcal per portion: 365
P = 17g, F = 18g, C = 33g*

PASTRY:
1 cup all-purpose flour
pinch of salt
2 tbsps sugar
1 egg
½ cup butter

FILLING:
5 cups low-fat small curd
  cottage cheese
⅔ cup sugar
1 tsp vanilla extract
2 tbsps vanilla custard
  powder or pudding mix
3 eggs, separated
⅔ cup heavy cream
2 tbsps currants
2 tbsps chopped almonds

fat or oil for the pan
1 egg yolk
2 tbsps milk

*Beat the cream into the cottage
cheese mixture.*

*Line the base and sides of a dish
with the rolled-out sweet
shortcrust pastry.*

*Whisk the egg yolk and milk and
brush the cheese filling with it.*

1. Sift the flour onto a pastry
board with the salt and sugar
and make a well in the middle. Break in the egg and
flake the chilled butter round
the edge. Chop everything
together with a chef's knife
then rapidly knead by hand
into a smooth dough. Wrap
in foil and leave in a cool
place for 30 minutes.
2. For the filling, put the cottage cheese in a bowl and
beat in the sugar, vanilla
extract, custard powder, and
egg yolk. Pour in the cream
and beat until smooth. Add
the currants and almonds.
Whisk the egg whites stiffly
and stir in evenly.
3. Pre-heat the oven of a
combination microwave
oven to 400°F.
4. Roll out the dough to a
round on a floured pastry
board and line the base and
sides of a greased micro-
wave cake pan 10 inches in
diameter.
5. Put the cottage cheese
mixture into the pastry case
and smooth flat. Whisk the
egg yolk and milk and brush
this glaze over the filling.
Bake on the middle shelf of
the oven for *25–30 minutes
at 180 Watts and 400°F (fan-
assisted model 375°F)* or
until golden. Leave to cool in
the cake pan.

PRUNE CAKE

SERVES 12 ■ ■
*Combination MW
Preparation and cooking
time: 50 minutes
Marinading time: 30 minutes
Kcal per portion: 405
P = 6g, F = 29g, C = 27g*

CAKE:
1½ cups pitted prunes
½ cup marsala or sweet red
  wine
⅔ cup butter or margarine
⅔ cup sugar
a pinch of salt
4 eggs, separated
6 tbsps ground walnuts
1 tsp baking powder
1 cup all-purpose flour
fat or oil for the dish

TOPPING:
1¾ cups heavy cream
2 tbsps vanilla sugar
6 medium plums
4 tbsps chopped walnuts

*Chop the prunes very finely and
marinate in marsala.*

*Fold the stiffly whisked egg whites
evenly into the prune cake
mixture.*

*Spread half the stiffly-whipped
cream over the cooled cake.*

1. Chop the prunes finely
with a chef's knife, put them
in a basin, and add the
marsala. Leave to marinade
for at least 30 minutes.
2. Pre-heat the oven of a
combination microwave
oven to 400°F.
3. Beat the softened fat,
sugar, and salt until creamy.
Gradually add the egg yolks,
beating constantly, then add
the flour mixed with the nuts
and baking powder. Stir in
the soaked prunes with their
liquid. Whisk the egg whites
very stiffly and fold in evenly.
4. Put the mixture into a
greased 10-inch cake pan
and bake on the middle shelf
of the oven for *20–25 minutes at 90 Watts and 400°F
(fan-assisted model 375°F)*.
Loosen the cake from the
pan and cool on a cake rack.
5. Add the vanilla sugar to
the cream, whip stiffly, and
use half of it to cover the top
and sides of the cake. Put the
rest in a piping bag and pipe
12 large rosettes round the
edge of the cake.

6. Rinse, dry, halve, and pit
the plums. Place half a plum,
cut side up, on each cream
rosette. Sprinkle with the
chopped walnuts.

ORANGE CAKE WITH KUMQUATS

SERVES 12 ■ ■
Combination MW
Preparation and cooking
time: 30 minutes
Kcal per portion: 330
P = 6g, F = 18g, C = 33g

2 oranges
⅔ cup butter or margarine,
    softened
⅔ cup sugar
1 tbsp vanilla sugar
grated rind of 1 orange
4 eggs, separated
2 tbsps Grand Marnier
¾ cup low-fat yogurt
1½ cups all-purpose flour
1 tsp baking powder
1 cup chopped almonds
fat or oil for the pan

2 cups kumquats
6 tbsps sugar
4 tbsps water
2 tbsps white rum

1. Peel the oranges with a sharp knife so deeply as to remove all the white parts. Loosen the flesh from the segment skins and cut into small pieces.
2. Pre-heat the oven of a combination microwave oven to 400°F.
3. Cream the softened fat with the sugar, vanilla sugar, and orange rind. Gradually add the egg yolk, liqueur, and yogurt. Mix together the flour, baking powder, and almonds and stir into the frothy mixture. Whisk the egg whites stiffly and fold evenly into the mixture with the orange pieces.
4. Put the mixture into a greased 10-inch cake pan and bake on the middle shelf of the oven for *12–15 minutes at 180 Watts and 400°F (fan-assisted model 375°F)* until golden.
5. Rinse the whole, unpeeled kumquats and slice them thinly. Stir the sugar, water, and rum

Cut the orange segments out of their individual skins using a sharp knife.

Fold the whisked egg whites and orange segments into the cake mixture.

Glaze the peeled and sliced kumquats with the syrup in the microwave.

together in a large microwave dish and after the cake is cooked, cook uncovered for *5–6 minutes at 600 Watts* to make a syrup. Add the sliced fruit and cook uncovered for a further *3–4 minutes at 600 Watts.*
6. When the cake has cooled, cover it with the glazed kumquats.

ORANGE POTATO CAKE

MAKES 12 ■
Combination MW
Preparation and cooking
time: 45 minutes
Kcal per portion: 215
P = 6g, F = 11g, C = 22g

50 raisins
3 tbsps Grand Marnier
2 medium potatoes boiled in
    their skins on the previous
    day
6 eggs, separated
¾ cup sugar
pinch of salt
grated rind of 1 orange
1½ cups ground almonds

fat or oil for the container
confectioner's sugar for
    dusting

1. Soak the raisins in the Grand Marnier. Pre-heat the oven of a combination microwave oven to 400°F.
2. Peel the potatoes and grate them finely.
3. Beat the egg yolks, sugar, and salt until thick and creamy. Stir in the orange rind, almonds, and potatoes. Whisk the egg whites stiffly and fold in evenly.
4. Put the mixture into a 10-inch cake pan and bake on the middle shelf for *18–22 minutes at 90 Watts and 400°F (fan-assisted model 375°F).*
5. Cool the cake on a rack. It can be dusted with confectioner's sugar through a paper lattice stencil if you wish; remove the stencil with care.

WHOLEFOOD PEAR CAKE WITH WALNUT TOPPING

Photograph on page 92/93

SERVES 12 ■ ■
Combination MW
Preparation and cooking
time: 1 hour
Kcal per portion: 345
P = 5g, F = 22g, C = 31

CAKE:
¾ cup butter
1 cup honey
3 eggs
2 cups whole-wheat cake
    flour
2 tsps baking powder
grated rind of ½ lemon
fat or oil for the container

TOPPING:
¼ cup butter
2 tbsps honey
1 cup chopped walnuts
½ tsp ground cinnamon
1 tbsp pear liqueur
8 medium ripe yellow pears

1. Beat the butter and honey until creamy and gradually add the eggs, the flour sifted with the baking powder, and the lemon rind. Put the mixture into a greased 9-inch cake pan.
2. For the topping, melt the butter and honey for 2 minutes at 600 Watts. Stir in the walnuts, cinnamon, and pear liqueur.
3. Pre-heat the oven of a combination microwave to 375°F.
4. Peel, quarter, and core the pears, cut them lengthwise into strips, and arrange them in a ring on the cake mixture. Spread the honey-and-nut mixture over them and bake on the lower shelf of the oven for *25–30 minutes at 180 Watts and 375°F (fan-assisted model 350°F) or* until golden-brown.
Serve with whipped cream.

CAPE GOOSEBERRY CAKE

SERVES 12　■
*Combination MW
Preparation and cooking
time: 30 minutes
Kcal per portion: 225
P = 4g, F = 14g, C = 21g*

CAKE:
⅔ cup butter or margarine,
　softened
⅔ cup sugar
grated rind and juice of 1
　lime
4 eggs, separated
4 tbsps chopped pistachios
4 tbsps vanilla wafer crumbs
4 tbsps all-purpose flour
fat or oil for the cake pan

TOPPING:
2 cups Cape gooseberries
　(physalis or Peruvian
　cherries)
confectioner's sugar for
　dusting

*Beat the softened fat with the
sugar, lime juice and rind until
creamy.*

*Gradually beat in the egg yolks,
then add the pistachios, vanilla
wafer crumbs, and flour.*

1. Pre-heat the oven of a
combination microwave
oven to 400°F.
2. Beat the fat with the sugar,
lime juice, and rind until
creamy. Gradually add the
egg yolks and the flour
mixed with the pistachios
and vanilla wafer crumbs.

TIP

*The Cape
gooseberries lend
the cake a
piquant acidity.*

*The papery calyx conceals
delicious fruit.*

Whisk the egg whites stiffly
and fold in evenly. Put the
mixture into a greased 10-
inch microwaveable pie pan.
3. Hull the Cape gooseberries and arrange them over
the cake mixture. Bake for
*14–16 minutes at 180 Watts
and 400°F (fan-assisted
model 175°F)* until golden-
brown. Allow to cool down a
little then dust with confectioner's sugar.

*Hull the Cape gooseberries and
arrange them on the uncooked
cake mixture.*

RHUBARB MERINGUE CAKE

SERVES 12　■ ■
*Combination MW
Preparation and cooking
time: 1 hour
Kcal per portion: 265
P = 4g, F = 13g, C = 33g*

CAKE:
⅔ cup butter
⅔ cup sugar
grated rind of ½ lemon
1 egg
2 egg yolks
1 cup all-purpose flour
4 tbsps cornstarch
1 tsp baking powder

TOPPING:
1¼ pounds rhubarb
2 egg whites
⅔ cup sugar
1 tsp lemon juice
4 tbsps chopped almonds

fat or oil for the cake pan

1. Beat the softened fat and
sugar until creamy.
Gradually add the lemon
rind, egg, and egg yolks,
beating all the time. Mix the
flour, cornstarch, and baking
powder and stir in. Beat
everything to a smooth mixture.

TIP

*Microwaves spare
us the pre-baking
of the mixture
with the rhubarb,
for the fast waves
cook the rhubarb
quickly and
gently, while the
temperature of
the baking oven
browns the cake.*

---

2. Pre-heat the oven of a
combination microwave to
375°F.
3. Rinse the sticks of
rhubarb, peel if necessary,
and cut into 1-inch pieces.

*Cream the fat and sugar, and
gradually beat in the lemon rind
and eggs.*

*Spread the meringue mixture
evenly over the rhubarb in the
cake pan.*

4. Whisk the egg whites
stiffly, add the sugar and
lemon juice, and continue to
whisk until the mixture is
smooth and firm. Lastly fold
in the almonds.
5. Put the mixture into a 10-
inch cake pan and arrange
the rhubarb evenly on top.
Spread the meringue mix-
ture over it or put it into a
piping bag with a large
round nozzle and pipe a lattice pattern over the top of
the cake.
6. Bake on the middle shelf
for *22–25 minutes at 180
Watts and 375°F (fan-assisted model 350°F)* until golden-brown. The cake tastes
best eaten fresh with
whipped cream. It will also
freeze excellently.

BANANA RING

SERVES 12 ■

Combination MW
Preparation and cooking
time: 45 minutes
Kcal per portion: 475
P = 7g, F = 27g, C = 50g

CAKE:
⅔ cup butter or margarine
⅔ cup sugar
1 tbsp vanilla sugar
4 eggs, separated
4 ripe bananas
4 tsps white rum
2 tsps baking powder
4 ounces baking chocolate,
   broken up
4 tbsps chopped filberts
   (hazelnuts)
2 cups all-purpose flour
fat or oil for the tube-pan

TOPPING:
4 ounces baking chocolate
1 cup heavy cream
12 dried banana slices
1 tbsp chopped pistachios

Ripe bananas are easily mashed with a fork.

Put the banana cake mixture into a greased tube-pan.

Pour the coating chocolate over the banana ring.

1. Pre-heat the oven of a combination microwave oven to 375°F.
2. Soften the fat, beat until creamy with the sugar and vanilla sugar, and gradually add the egg yolks.
3. Peel the bananas, mash with a fork, and add the rum. Combine the flour, baking powder, chocolate, and nuts and add gradually to the creamy mixture, alternately with the bananas. Whisk the egg whites stiffly and fold in evenly.
4. Grease a 9-inch microwaveable tube-pan, add the mixture, and bake on the middle shelf for *25–30 minutes at 180 Watts and 350°F (fan-assisted model 325°F)*. Turn the cake out onto a rack and leave to cool a little.
5. Break up the coating chocolate, put it in a shallow basin, and melt for *1–2 minutes at 600 Watts*. Stir well, then coat the cake with it and leave to set.
6. Before serving, whip the cream stiffly, put it in a piping bag, and decorate the cake with rosettes. Stick a banana slice in each and sprinkle with the pistachios. The cake tastes best if eaten the following day. If it is to be kept longer, omit the whipped cream decoration.

MANGO FLAN WITH COCONUT CRUST

SERVES 12 ■■

Combination MW
Preparation and cooking
time: 30 minutes
Resting time: 30 minutes
Kcal per portion: 350
P = 5g, f = 20g, C = 37g

PASTRY:
2 cups all-purpose flour
4 tbsps cornstarch
pinch of salt
4 tbsps sugar
grated rind of ½ lemon
2 egg yolks
⅔ cup butter

FILLING:
2 medium-sized ripe mangoes
3 eggs, separated
⅓ cup sugar
2 tbsps crème fraîche or sour
   cream
4 tsps coconut liqueur or
   pina colada
1 cup flaked coconut

fat or oil for the container

Peel the mangoes, remove the stones, and slice thinly.

Beat the coconut thoroughly with the egg-and-sugar mixture.

Spread the coconut cream evenly over the mango filling.

1. Sift the flour and cornstarch onto a pastry board, mix with the salt, sugar, and lemon rind, make a well in the middle, put in the egg yolks, and flake the chilled butter round the edge. Chop everything together with a chef's knife, then rapidly knead by hand into a smooth dough. Wrap in foil and leave in a cool place for 30 minutes.
2. Meanwhile, peel the mangoes and cut the flesh off the stone in thin slices.
3. Pre-heat the oven of a combination microwave oven to 400°F.
4. Beat the egg yolks and sugar until thick and creamy. Mix in the crème fraîche or sour cream, liqueur, and coconut flakes. Whisk the egg white stiffly and fold in.
5. Flour a pastry board and roll out the sweet shortcrust dough to a circle. Grease a 10-inch microwaveable cake pan and line the base and sides with the pastry. Prick all over with a fork.
6. Arrange the mango slices in a circle on the pastry base and cover evenly with the coconut cream, then bake on the bottom shelf for *15–18 minutes at 180 Watts and 400°F (fan-assisted model 375°F)* or until crisp and golden.

POPPYSEED SLICE WITH PEARS

SERVES 15 ■ ■ ■
Combination MW
Preparation and cooking
time: 50 minutes
Resting time: 30 minutes
Kcal per portion: 485
P = 13g, F = 27g, C = 47g

PASTRY:
2 cups all-purpose flour
pinch of salt
1 tsp baking powder
4 tbsps sugar
1 egg yolk
⅔ cup butter

POPPYSEED FILLING:
2 cups freshly ground
* poppyseeds*
2 tbsps farina (cream of
* wheat)*
1 cup milk
½ cup heavy cream
½ cup butter
½ cup sugar
2 tbsps raisins

COTTAGE CHEESE TOPPING:
2 eggs, separated
½ cup sugar
grated rind of 1 lemon
2 cups small-curd cottage
* cheese*
4 tbsps melted butter

FRUIT TOPPING:
pears (e.g. Bartlett, Comice,
* Bose)*
4 tbsps flaked almonds
2 tbsps confectioner's sugar

1. Sift the flour onto a pastry board and mix with salt, baking powder, and sugar. Make a well in the middle, put the egg yolk in it, and flake the chilled butter round the edge. Chop everything together with a chef's knife then rapidly knead by hand into a smooth dough. Wrap in foil and leave in a cool place for 30 minutes.
2. Mix the poppyseed and farina in a basin. Heat the milk, cream, butter, and sugar in another basin for

Pour the hot cream, butter, and sugar into the poppyseed and farina, and add the raisins.

Lay the pear slices like roof tiles on the poppyseed filling.

2–3 minutes at 600 Watts then beat into the poppyseed mixture. Add the raisins.
3. For the cottage cheese filling, beat the egg yolks with sugar and lemon rind until frothy, then spoon in the cottage cheese and melted butter. Whisk the egg whites stiffly and fold in evenly.
4. Peel, halve, and core the pears and slice them thinly lengthwise.
5. Pre-heat the oven of a combination microwave to 450°F.
6. Flour a pastry board, roll out the pastry to a 12x14-inch rectangle and lay it on a baking sheet. Prick with a fork, spread with the cottage cheese mixture, then the poppyseed mixture. Arrange the sliced pears on top, and sprinkle with flaked almonds and confectioner's sugar.
7. Bake the poppyseed slice for *25–30 minutes at 180 Watts and 450°F (fan-assisted model 400°F).*

MERINGUE CASES

MAKES 30 ■
Conventional MW
Preparation and cooking
time: 20 minutes
Kcal per portion: 55
P = 0g, F = 0g, C = 13g

1 egg white
3 cups confectioner's sugar
grated rind of ½ a lemon
strawberry cream, chocolate
* cream or ice cream*

1. Beat the egg white with a fork until light and frothy, gradually beat in the sifted confectioner's sugar and the lemon rind, and knead in the rest.
2. Dust the worktop with confectioner's sugar and shape the mixture, first to a roll then into 30 balls about 1-inch across. Lay 10 balls at a time, widely spaced, on a baking sheet lined with non-stick baking parchment – the meringues double in size when cooked.
3. Place each sheetful in the microwave for *3½–4 minutes at 600 Watts.* Bake for about 5 minutes before removing them from the paper and placing them on a rack to cool. Sandwich the meringues in pairs with strawberry cream, chocolate cream, or ice cream.
4. Finish by cooking, covered, for *4 minutes at 360 Watts,* then uncovered for *5–6 minutes at 600 Watts.* Leave to cool on the plate then dust thickly with confectioner's sugar and serve with whipped cream.

SPICE CAKE

SERVES 12 ■
Conventional MW
Preparation and cooking
time: 25 minutes
Kcal per portion: 215
P = 4g, F = 12g, C = 23g

½ cup butter or margarine
½ cup sugar
3 eggs, separated
grated rind of 1 orange
1 tsp ground cinnamon
½ tsp ground ginger
pinch of ground clove
pinch of ground nutmeg
pinch of ground allspice
4 tsps orange liqueur
4 tbsps ground filberts
* (hazelnuts)*
1 tbsp cocoa powder
4 tbsps cornstarch
1 tsp baking powder
1 cup all-purpose flour

fat or oil for the container
confectioner's sugar for
* dusting*

1. Soften the fat and beat with the sugar until creamy. Gradually add the egg yolks, spices, and orange liqueur, beating all the time. Mix the nuts, cocoa, cornstarch, baking powder, and flour and stir in. Whisk the egg whites stiffly and fold in evenly.

> **TIP**
>
> *Cakes cooked in a conventional microwave oven taste best when fresh.*

2. Grease a 9-inch microwaveable cake pan, pour in the cake mixture, and smooth the top. Cook uncovered for *4 minutes at 600 Watts and 4–5 minutes at 600 Watts.* Leave to cool in the container.
3. Tip out onto a cake rack and dust thickly with confectioner's sugar.

BAKED APPLES IN PUFF PASTRY

MAKES 4 ■■
Combination MW
Preparation and cooking
time: 40 minutes
Kcal per portion: 420
P = 6g, F = 25g, C = 42g

10 ounces frozen puff dough
4 small cooking apples
   (Gravenstein, Rome
   Beauty, or Rhode Island
   Greening)
2 tbsps marmalade
2 tbsps flaked almonds
1 tsp chopped candied
   orange peel
1 egg yolk
1 tbsp milk

1. Place the slabs of frozen pastry side by side and thaw for *2-3 minutes at 180 Watts.*
2. Peel and core the apples. Mix the marmalade with the almonds, ginger, and candied peel.
3. Pre-heat a combination microwave to 425°F.
4. Brush the pastry slabs with a little water, lay one on top of another, roll out to a thickness of about ¹⁄₁₀ inch, and cut into 4 squares. Set an apple in the center of each and fill the hole with the marmalade mixture. Pull up the corners of the dough so that the apples are completely encased. From the dough scraps, make small stars or rounds and use a little water to stick them on top of the pastry cases.
5. Prick the pastry all over with a fork. Beat the egg yolk and milk together and use it to brush the pastry.
6. Place the wrapped apples on a tray lined with nonstick baking parchment and bake on the middle shelf for *9–11 minutes at 180 Watts and 450°F (fan-assisted model 400°F)* until golden-brown.

WALNUT BREAD

MAKES 20 SLICES ■■
Combination MW
Preparation and cooking
time: 45 minutes
Rising time: 1 hour 45 minutes
Kcal per portion: 115
P = 4g, F = 8g, C = 17g

DOUGH:
1¾ cups fine whole-wheat
   flour
4 tbsps wheat berries
1 tsp salt
3 tbsps fresh yeast
pinch of sugar
1 cup lukewarm water
5 tbsps olive oil
1 cup walnuts, coarsely
   chopped

3–4 tbsps milk for brushing

1. Mix the whole-wheat flour, wheat grains, and salt in a basin, make a well in the middle, and crumble in the yeast. Sprinkle with sugar and work into a starter dough with some of the water and flour. Cover and leave to rise in a warm place for 15 minutes.
2. Pour in the remaining water and the oil and knead, preferably by hand, on a floured board, until the dough is smooth and shiny. Cover and leave to rise in a

> ### TIP
> *The time saved in baking is about 30 minutes.*

warm place for about 1 hour, until it has doubled in volume.
3. Knead the dough again vigorously, add the nuts, and knead them in well. Shape into a round loaf, cover, and leave on the floured board to rise for another 30 minutes.
4. Pre-heat the oven of a combination microwave oven to 400°F.

Always leave chopping walnuts until the last minute, so that they retain their flavor.

In a well in the flour, mix the yeast, sugar, water, and flour into a starter dough.

Knead the chopped walnuts into the dough before it rests for the last time.

5. Brush the loaf with milk and bake on the bottom shelf for *30–35 minutes at 90 Watts and 400°F (fan-assisted model 375°F)* until golden brown.
The loaf can be decorated before baking with chopped or halved walnuts, if desired.

PEACH TARTLETS

MAKES 4 ■
Combination MW
Preparation and cooking
time: 25 minutes
Kcal per portion: 245
P = 4g, F = 15g, C = 23g

10 ounces frozen puff dough
2 ripe peaches
1 tbsp lemon marmalade
1 tsp white rum
20g toasted flaked almonds

1. Place the slabs of dough side-by-side and thaw for *2-3 minutes at 180 Watts.*
2. Pre-heat the oven of a combination microwave oven to 450°F.
3. Blanch, peel, halve, and pit the peaches and slice thinly.
4. Brush the slabs of dough with some water, lay one on top of another, and roll out to about ½ inch thick. Cut out 4 rounds about 4 inches across and lay them on a tray lined with nonstick baking parchment. Fan the peach slices round on top of them.
5. Bake the tartlets on the middle shelf for *8–10 minutes at 180 Watts and 450°F (fan-assisted model 400°F).*
6. Stir the marmalade and rum together and after the tartlets are cooked, heat for *1 minute at 600 Watts.* Glaze the peaches and the edges of the pastry with this and sprinkle the toasted, flaked almonds round the edges.

Lean Cuisine

*E*ven if you have gone on a
slimming diet, there is no
need to deny yourself sweet
things from your own oven.
The recipes in this chapter do
not compromise on good
flavor. Apricot Sponge Flan
with Sunflower Seeds, Apple
and Lime Roll, and the ever
popular spongecakes are
particularly economical on
calories but substantial,
sweet, and mouth-watering.
Other nourishing patisserie,
such as Raspberry Dome
Cake and Mango Flan, are by
no means calorie bombs. You
will even find recipes for
Sponge Fingers which are not
excessively high in calories.

Mixed Berry Flan
(see recipe on page 118)

EXOTIC YOGURT CAKE

SERVES 12 ■■
Preparation and cooking time: 1 hour
Resting time: a few hours
Kcal per portion: 170
P = 7g, F = 6g, C = 22g

SPONGE BASE:
2 eggs, separated
2 tbsps water
3 tbsps sugar
2 tbsps cornstarch
½ tsp baking powder
4 tbsps all-purpose flour

TOPPING:
5 tbsps powdered gelatin
1 ripe mango
4 kiwis
sweetener according to taste
1 egg white
4 tsps sugar
4 tsps orange liqueur
1½ cups low-fat yogurt
2 tbsps kiwi-fruit jam
2 tbsps chopped pistachios

1. Pre-heat oven to 400°F.
2. Whisk the egg whites with water until stiff and gradually sprinkle in the sugar. Continue whisking until the mixture is firm and shiny. Then stir in the egg yolks gradually and the flour mixed with cornstarch and baking powder.
3. Line a 9-inch springform pan with nonstick baking parchment, put in the sponge mixture, and bake on the middle shelf of the oven for about 25 minutes.
4. Turn the cake out onto a rack and peel off the paper. Leave to cool, then cut in half horizontally and reserve one half for a future recipe.
5. For the topping, soak the gelatin in cold water. Peel and dice the mango and kiwi fruits and add sweetener to taste.
6. Whisk the egg whites stiffly, sprinkling in the sugar. Warm the orange liqueur, and dissolve the powdered gelatin in it.

Combine the stiffly whisked egg white, the whipped cream, and the yogurt mixture.

Spread jam on the sponge base then put the ring of the springform pan in place.

7. Beat the yogurt and gradually add the dissolved gelatin, beating all the time. Leave to set in the refrigerator or a basin surrounded by iced water. As soon as it starts to set, stir in the egg whites and fruit.
8. Spread the cake base with jam, place it on the base of the springform pan and add the ring. Fill with the yogurt mixture and leave to set in the refrigerator for several hours.
9. Release the cake from the springform and decorate with the pistachios.
Add any further decoration you fancy, such as sliced kiwi fruits.

BUCKWHEAT CAKE WITH CRANBERRIES

SERVES 12 ■■
Preparation and cooking time: 1 hour
Kcal per portion: 190
P = 4g, F = 10g, C = 19g

4 eggs, separated
4 tbsps sugar
4 tsps raspberry liqueur
1 cup fine buckwheat flour
4 tbsps filberts (hazelnuts), toasted and ground
1 tsp baking powder
2 tbsps melted butter
1¼ cups fresh cranberries
grated rind and juice of 1 orange
sweetener according to taste
confectioner's sugar for dusting
½ cup heavy cream
1 tbsp chopped pistachios for decoration

1. Pre-heat the oven to 350°F.
2. Beat the egg yolks, sugar, and raspberry liqueur together until thick and creamy. Gradually add the buckwheat flour, the ground hazelnuts, and the baking powder. Whisk the egg whites stiffly and fold into the mixture.
3. Line the base of a 9-inch springform pan with non-stick baking parchment, put in the cake mixture, and bake on the middle shelf of the oven for 35–40 minutes. Release the cake from the pan and leave to cool on a cake rack.
4. Meanwhile, sort and wash the cranberries and drain them in a sieve. Put them in a saucepan with the orange juice and rind and reduce to a thick mass over a medium heat for 15–20 minutes. Add sweetener to taste, remove from the heat, and leave in a cool place.
5. Slice the cake in half horizontally. Spread cranberry

Cook the cranberries to a thick mass with orange juice and sweetener.

Slice the cooled sponge in half and fill it with the cranberry mixture.

Put a spot of cranberry mixture on each rosette of cream.

mixture on the bottom layer, reserving a couple of spoonfuls for decoration. Place the upper layer on top and dust thickly with confectioner's sugar.
6. Whip the cream stiffly, put it in a piping bag with a star-shaped nozzle, and pipe 12 rosettes round the edge of the cake. Dot each with a little remaining cranberry mixture and sprinkle with pistachios, if liked.

RASPBERRY DOME
CAKE

RASPBERRY DOME CAKE

SERVES 12 ■ ■ ■

*Preparation and cooking
time: 30 minutes
Resting time: a few hours
Kcal per portion: 290
P = 16g, F = 6g, C = 42g*

*24 sponge fingers
juice of 1 lemon*

*Line a basin with moistened
sponge fingers.*

FILLING:

*4 tbsps powdered gelatin
½ cup raspberries
sweetener according to taste
2 egg whites
2 tbsps sugar
3 cups quark or small-curd
    cottage cheese
⅔ cup cream
2 tbsps raspberry liqueur
few mint leaves*

1. Soak half the sponge fin-gers in enough lemon juice to make them pliable, then use them to line a dome mold or round-bottomed basin 8 inches across, stand-ing them upright, side-by-side.

2. Soften the gelatin in 2 tbsps cold water. Sort the raspberries, purée half of them, sieve, and add sweet-ener.

3. Whisk the egg whites stiffly, gradually sprinkling in the sugar. Beat until the mix-ture is firm and shiny. Whip the cream stiffly in another basin. Squeeze out the gelatin, warm the raspberry liqueur, and dissolve the powdered gelatin in it.

4. Beat the quark or cottage cheese and gradually add the raspberry pulp and dis-solved gelatin, beating all the time. Fold in the beaten egg white and cream. Reserve 2 tablespoons of the mixture then mix the fruit into the rest, reserving some for dec-orating.

5. Fill the lined dome mold with the raspberry cream and top with the remaining sponge fingers. Leave in a

*Fill with the raspberry mixture
and leave in a cool place for
several hours.*

*Arrange remaining sponge fingers
attractively on the top.*

cool place for several hours.
6. Turn the cake out onto a serving dish and decorate with the reserved cream and fruit, and the mint leaves. Serve well chilled.

Strawberries may be used in place of raspberries for this recipe.

PEAR GÂTEAU

SERVES 10 ■ ■

*Preparation and cooking
time: 45 minutes
Resting time: 2 hours
Kcal per portion: 195
P = 6g, F = 9g, C = 20g*

FILLING:

*pears (e.g. Bose, Comice)
1 cup water
piece of fresh ginger root
½ cinnamon stick
4 cloves
rind of 1 lemon
5 tbsps powdered gelatin
1 tbsp pear liqueur
sweetener to taste*

BASE:

*30 vanilla wafers or sponge
    cookies
3 tbsps butter
4 tsps pear liqueur*

TOPPING:

*½ cup cream
1 tbsp flaked chocolate*

1. Peel, halve and core the pears, and slice thinly. Bring the water and spices to the boil, put in the sliced pears, cover, and cook until soft.
2. Soak the gelatin in cold water.
3. Select 5 nice slices of pear and reserve them for the top-ping. Lift out the spices and purée the pears and liquid in a food processor. Dissolve the powdered gelatin in the hot purée, flavor with sweet-ener and pear liqueur, and leave to cool.
4. Meanwhile, crumble the wafers or cookies in the food processor, reserve 2 table-spoons, and work the rest into the softened butter and liqueur to form a pliable mix-ture.
5. Lay a 9-inch pie pan on a cake platter and fill the bot-tom with the cookie mixture. Sprinkle with the reserved crumbs. Spread the pear purée on top and leave to set in the refrigerator.
6. Whip the cream stiffly and put into a piping bag.

*Peel and core the pears and cut
evenly into thin slices.*

*Cook the pears until soft in 1 cup
water with the spices.*

*Purée the cooked pears finely in a
blender.*

Decorate the gâteau with rosettes and sprinkle with the flaked chocolate. Arrange the reserved pear slices between the cream rosettes. Allow to chill well before serving.

APRICOT SPONGE FLAN WITH SUN-FLOWER SEEDS

SERVES 12 ■
Preparation and cooking time: 1 hour
Kcal per portion: 120
P = 4g, F = 3g, C = 18g

3 cups apricots
3 eggs, separated
2 tbsps sugar
juice and grated rind of
    1 lemon
1 package custard powder or
    vanilla pudding mix
4 tbsps cookie crumbs
1 tsp baking powder
4 tbsps all-purpose flour
2 tbsps sunflower seeds

The cake tastes particularly good if made with fresh ripe apricots.

1. Pre-heat the oven to 400°F. Rinse, halve, and pit the apricots.
2. Whisk the egg whites stiffly, gradually add the

Whisk the whites of 3 eggs stiffly until firm and shiny.

TIP

When whisking egg white stiffly, it is essential that the basin be completely free of fat.

sugar, lemon juice and rind, and beat until the mixture is firm and shiny.
3. Combine the flour, custard powder, cookie crumbs, and baking powder, then stir the egg yolks and the flour mixture into the egg white mixture.
4. Line a 10-inch springform pan with nonstick baking parchment, fill with the mixture, and top with the drained apricots, cut-side downward. Sprinkle with sunflower seeds.
5. Bake on the middle shelf of the oven for 30–35 minutes.
6. Release the cake from the springform and leave to cool on a cake rack.

Beat all the rest of the ingredients for the base into the egg whites.

Before cooking, decorate the cake with the apricot halves and sprinkle with the sunflower seeds.

QUARK CAKE WITH SOUR CHERRIES

SERVES 12 ■ ■
Preparation and cooking time: 1 hour
Resting time: 3 hours
Kcal per portion: 175
P = 11g, F = 5g, c = 22g

BASE:
2 eggs, separated
2 tbsps water
3 tbsps sugar
2 tbsps cornstarch
½ tsp baking powder
4 tbsps all-purpose flour

FILLING:
2 cups sour cherries
2 tbsps powdered gelatin
2 cups quark
sweetener to taste
2 egg whites
¾ ounce sugar
⅔ cup heavy cream

confectioner's sugar for dusting

1. Pre-heat the oven to 400°F.
2. Whisk the egg whites and water until stiff, then gradually sprinkle in the sugar. Continue beating until the mixture is firm and shiny. Beat in the egg yolks. Combine the cornstarch, baking powder, and flour and gradually stir into the egg mixture.
3. Line the base of a 9-inch springform pan with nonstick baking parchment, fill with the sponge mixture, smooth flat, and bake on the middle shelf of the oven for about 25 minutes. Release the cake from the springform and leave to cool on a rack.
4. For the filling, rinse and pit the cherries. Soak the gelatin in cold water. Put the quark in a basin, sweeten to taste, and beat until smooth. Dissolve powdered gelatine in 3 tbsps hot water, then stir it into the quark.
5. Whisk the egg whites

Spread the cream and quark mixture evenly over the pitted cherries.

Lay the other half of the sponge base on top of the smoothed cream.

stiffly, sprinkling with the sugar. In another basin, whip the cream and fold them both gently into the quark.
6. Slice the cake base horizontally and lay one half back in the springform pan. Arrange the cherries on it and cover with the quark mixture. Smooth the top and cover with the other half of the cake. Leave to set in the refrigerator for about 3 hours.
7. Release the cake from the springform, dust with confectioner's sugar and serve well chilled. If canned cherries are used, they must be well drained beforehand. Instead of cherries, the cake can be filled with peaches or apricots.

FRUIT STAR

SERVES 12 ■■

*Preparation and cooking
time: 1 hour
Kcal per portion: 185
P = 4g, F = 6g, C = 26g*

PASTRY:
*½ cup small-curd cottage
    cheese
2 tbsps sugar
4 tbsps sunflower oil
4 tbsps milk
grated rind of ½ a lemon
2 tsps baking powder
2 cups all-purpose flour*

TOPPING:
*4 ripe kiwis
4 cups strawberries
1 cup dry white wine
1 package jelly glaze or
    4 tsps potato starch
sweetener to taste*

1. Pre-heat the oven to 375°F.
2. Mix the flour and baking powder. Combine the cottage cheese, sugar, oil, milk, and lemon rind and gradually add the flour. Flour a pastry board, knead the dough, and roll it out ¼ inch thick. Cut out a 12-point star 14 inches across. Line a baking sheet with nonstick baking parchment and lay the star on it. Gather together the offcuts and make a smaller star about 3 inches across. Bake both on the middle shelf of the oven for 15–20 minutes.
3. Peel the kiwis and slice them thinly. Rinse, hull, and halve the strawberries. When the pastry has cooled, decorate the larger star with alternate rings of the prepared kiwis and strawberries.
4. Take 3 tablespoons of the white wine and mix it with the jelly glaze or potato starch. Bring the rest of the wine to the boil and stir in the dissolved powder. Sweeten to taste and pour over the fruit. Lay the small star right in the center.

Kiwis are among the most decorative of exotic fruits and are widely available

Cut the pastry star out on the baking sheet with the help of a paper pattern.

Arrange sliced kiwis and halved strawberries alternately on the cooked pastry.

The glaze is prepared with white wine, which gives that extra zing.

FRUITY SPONGE CAKE

SERVES 12 ■

*Preparation and cooking
time: 1 hour 20 minutes
Kcal per portion: 200
P = 4g, F = 9g, C = 25g*

*1 ripe mango (about 1 cup
    fruit pulp)
sweetener to taste
½ cup butter or margarine
2 tbsps sugar
3 eggs
grated rind and juice of 1
    orange
2 tsps baking powder
4 tbsps cornstarch
2 cups all-purpose flour*

*fat or oil for the pan
confectioner's sugar for
    dusting*

1. Peel the mango and slice the flesh from the stone, purée it, and sweeten to taste.
2. Pre-heat the oven to 350°F.
3. Sift together the flour, cornstarch, and baking powder. Soften the fat, and cream it with the sugar. Gradually add the eggs, orange rind and juice, mango purée, and flour, beating all the time.
4. Grease a tube-pan or Bundt pan, fill with the cake mixture, and bake on the bottom shelf of the oven for about 1 hour 10 minutes, or until golden-brown. Turn out onto a rack and allow to cool. Dust lightly with confectioner's sugar. If you are not strictly weight-watching, add some freshly ground pinenuts to the mixture.

RHUBARB CAKE

SERVES 12 ■

*Preparation and cooking
time: 1 hour
Marinading time: 30 minutes
Kcal per portion: 160
P = 3g, F = 9g, C = 15g*

*1¼ pounds rhubarb
sweetener to taste
4 tsps orange liqueur
½ cup butter or margarine
6 tbsps sugar
2 eggs separated
grated rind of ½ an orange
4 tbsps flour
4 tbsps breadcrumbs
1 tsp baking powder
fat or oil for the pan
2 tbsps flaked almonds*

1. Peel the rhubarb if necessary, cut into ½-inch pieces and put in a basin. Add sweetener and liqueur, cover and leave to marinade for about 30 minutes.
2. Pre-heat the oven to 350°F.

TIP

This cake can be cooked in a combination microwave oven in about 17 minutes.

3. Soften the fat, cream it with the sugar, and add the egg yolks, orange rind, flour, breadcrumbs, and baking powder. Whisk the egg whites stiffly and stir into the mixture.
4. Grease a 9-inch springform pan and put in the cake mixture. Spread the rhubarb with its liquid over the mixture and sprinkle with the almonds.
5. Bake the rhubarb cake for about 45 minutes on the bottom shelf of the oven.

MANGO FLAN

SERVES 12 ■■
*Preparation and cooking
time: 45 minutes
Resting time: 2 hours
Kcal per portion: 235
P = 6g, F = 12g, C = 25g*

BASE:
*4 ounces small-curd cottage
  cheese
30g/1oz sugar
4 tbsps sunflower oil
3 tbsps milk
1 tsp vanilla extract
1 cup all-purpose flour
1 tsp baking powder*

FILLING:
*3 medium-sized, ripe
  mangoes
3 tbsps Grand Marnier
2 tbsps powdered gelatin
sweetener to taste*

*fat or oil for the pan
dried beans for blind baking
2 tbsps powdered gelatin
½ cup heavy cream
chopped pistachios*

*Peel the mangoes and cut the
flesh off the large flat stone.*

*Line the dough base with
nonstick baking parchment and
dried beans.*

1. Pre-heat the oven to 400°F.
2. Beat together the cottage cheese, sugar, oil, milk, and the vanilla extract. Mix the flour and baking powder and add to the mixture. Knead the dough on a

TIP

*The cake base can
well be made in
advance. It will
keep several days
if wrapped in
aluminum foil.
Fill it a few hours
before serving.
Alternatively, it
can be sprinkled
with pinenuts.*

floured pastry board, then roll out to a round 12 inches in diameter.
3. Grease a 10-inch springform pan and line with the dough, making a rim 1 inch high. Line with nonstick baking parchment, scatter dried beans over the bottom, and bake on the middle shelf of the oven for 15–20 minutes. Remove the paper and beans, and leave to cool.
4. For the filling, peel the mangoes, cut the flesh off the stone, and purée it in a food processor. Warm the Grand Marnier, dissolve the powdered gelatin in it, and stir in the fruit purée. Sweeten to taste.
5. Spread the mango purée over the base and leave in a cool place until set.
6. Whip the cream stiffly, put it in a piping bag, and decorate the edge of the cake as shown in the illustration. Sprinkle with pistachios and chocolate sprinkles if liked.

MIXED BERRY FLAN

Photograph on page
108/109

SERVES 10 ■■
*Preparation and cooking
time: 50 minutes
Kcal per portion: 170
P = 4g, F = 8g, C = 17g*

PASTRY:
*1 cup all-purpose flour
pinch of salt
1 tbsp sugar
2 tbsps ground almonds
½ cup small-curd cottage
  cheese
4 tbsps butter*

FILLING:
*3 cups mixed fresh soft fruit
  (e.g. strawberries,
  blueberries, blackcurrants,
  raspberries, blackberries)
1 cup dry red wine
1 packet instant jelly glaze
sweetener to taste*

*fat or oil for the pan
dried beans for blind baking
1 tbsp flaked almonds*

1. Sift the flour onto a pastry board and mix with the salt, sugar, and almonds. Flake the chilled butter on top, add the cheese and chop together with a chef's knife, then knead by hand to a smooth dough.
2. Pre-heat the oven to 400°F.
3. Roll the dough out to a round 11 inches across. Grease a 9-inch springform pan and line the base and sides with the dough. Line the bottom with nonstick baking parchment, scatter some dried beans on it, and bake on the middle shelf of the oven for 25 minutes.
4. Sort the fruit, rinse if necessary, and halve any large berries. Remove the beans and paper from the cooked base and leave it to cool a little before arranging the fruit on it.

*Pick the blackcurrants carefully
from their stalks and rinse
quickly.*

*Briskly chop together all the
pastry ingredients with a chef's
knife.*

*Knead by hand to a smooth
dough and roll into a ball.*

5. Take 3 tablespoons of the red wine and mix the cake glaze with it. Bring the rest of the wine to the boil and pour in the mixed powder, stirring all the time. Sweeten and pour over the fruit. Sprinkle the edge with the flaked almonds. Serve well chilled with low-fat plain yogurt. The same flan can be made with one sort of fruit alone.

FRUIT TARTS

MAKES 10 ■■
*Preparation and cooking
time: 50 minutes
Rising time: 1 hour
Kcal per portion: 225
P = 5g, F = 8g, C = 34g*

PASTRY:
*2 cups all-purpose flour
pinch of salt
2 tbsps fresh yeast or 1
    package dry yeast
½ cup (at least) lukewarm
    milk
1 tbsp sugar
4 tbsps melted butter or
    margarine
fat or oil for the pan*

FILLINGS:
*5 cups fruit of your choice
    e.g. cherries, apricots,
    raspberries, strawberries,
    or apples
2 tbsps apricot jam
2 tbsps toasted flaked
    almonds*

Before dividing up the yeast dough give it another thorough kneading.

Cut the dough into 10 portions and press by hand into small tart shapes.

Arrange the fruit on the tarts and leave to rise for a further 15 minutes.

1. Mix the flour and salt in a basin and make a well in the middle. Crumble in the yeast and mix to a starter dough with half the milk, ½ tsp sugar, and 2–3 tbsps flour. Cover and leave to rise in a warm place for 15 minutes.
2. Add the melted fat and work all the ingredients into a smooth dough, continuing to knead until it no longer sticks to the bowl. Cover and leave to rise in a warm place for a further 30 minutes.
3. To prepare the fruit, pit cherries and apricots, rinse raspberries and strawberries, peel, core, and slice apples.
4. Pre-heat the oven to 400°F.
5. Knead the dough again briefly on a floured pastry board and cut into 10 pieces. Shape each into a round 4 inches across with a thicker edge. Lay 5 at a time on a floured baking sheet, fill with fruit and leave to rise for a further 15 minutes.
6. Bake one batch at a time on the middle shelf for about

25 minutes. Warm the apricot jam in a small saucepan and use it to brush over the fruit and the pastry edges. Sprinkle the flaked almonds round the edges.

APPLE AND LIME ROLL

SERVES 15 ■■
*Preparation and cooking
time: 45 minutes
Kcal per portion: 135
P = 7g, F = 5g, C = 16g*

SPONGE:
*1 large cooking apple
grated rind and juice of ½ a
    lime
4 eggs, separated
6 tbsps sugar
4 tsps Calvados or applejack
4 tbsps all-purpose flour
2 tbsps cornstarch
½ tsp baking powder
sugar for dusting*

FILLING:
*2 large cooking apples
2 limes
2 cups small-curd cottage
    cheese
liquid sweetener to taste
½ cup plain yogurt*

1. Peel the apples, grate them finely, and mix with the lime juice and rind.
2. Pre-heat the oven to 400°F.
3. Beat the egg yolks, sugar, and Calvados until thick and creamy. Add the flour, cornstarch, and baking powder and stir into the mixture. Whisk the egg whites stiffly and fold them and the grated apple evenly into the mixture.
4. Line a baking sheet with nonstick baking parchment, spread the sponge mixture on it, and bake on the middle shelf of the oven for about 12 minutes or until golden. Turn it out onto a kitchen towel sprinkled with sugar, dampen the paper, and peel it off. Roll up the sponge with the cloth and leave to cool.
5. Meanwhile, for the filling, peel the apples and grate coarsely. Mix with the juice and grated rind of a rinsed lime. Beat the cheese until smooth and sweeten to

Roll up the baked sponge while hot with the help of a kitchen towel.

When the sponge roll has cooled, unroll it and spread it with the cream.

taste. Whip the cream stiffly and fold into the cheese. Set aside one-third of this and mix the rest with the grated apples.
6. Unroll the sponge roll and spread with the apple-and-cheese mixture. Roll it up again, still with the help of the kitchen towel, and lay it, seam downward, on a long dish.
7. Pile the remaining cheese mixture on top of the roll and draw lines along it with a fork. Rinse the second lime, shave off the rind with a lemon zester and use this to decorate the top of the roll.

SPONGE FINGERS

MAKES 20 ■
*Preparation and cooking
time: 30 minutes
Kcal per portion: 55
P = 1g, F = 1g, C =10g*

3 eggs, separated
2 tbsps sugar
pinch of salt
1 tsp vanilla extract
1 tsp lemon juice
3 tbsps cornstarch
4 tbsps all-purpose flour
confectioner's sugar for
    dusting

1. Pre-heat the oven to 350°F.
2. Beat the egg yolk, 1 table-spoon sugar, and the vanilla extract until thick and frothy. Whisk the egg whites until stiff and gradually add the

Run freshly squeezed lemon juice slowly into the sponge mixture.

Pipe the fingers onto the baking sheet with good gaps between them.

Dust the fingers with confectioner's sugar before baking.

> ### TIP
>
> *Sponge fingers can be kept for several days in a tin.*

salt, remaining sugar, and lemon juice. Continue beating until the mixture is firm and shiny.
3. Heap the egg white onto the yolk mixture, sift the flour and cornstarch together on top and mix well.
4. Put the mixture into a piping bag with a large round nozzle, and pipe strips about 3 inches long and thicker at the ends, onto a baking sheet lined with nonstick baking parchment. Leave plenty of room between the fingers as they tend to spread. Dust with confectioner's sugar and bake on the middle shelf of the oven for about 10 minutes.
5. Loosen the fingers from the paper immediately with a metal spatula and leave them to cool.

LEMON SLICE

SERVES 10 ■ ■
*Preparation and cooking
time: 50 minutes
Kcal per portion: 190
P = 4g, F = 6g, C = 30g*

SPONGE:
3 eggs, separated
6 tbsps sugar
grated rind of 1 lemon
1 cup all-purpose flour
sugar for sprinkling

FILLING:
1 cup freshly squeezed lemon
    juice (3–4 lemons)
1 cup water
½ cup cornstarch
1 egg, separated
2 tbsps sugar
sweetener to taste

DECORATION:
½ cup heavy cream
3 slices of lemon
20 small leaves of lemon
    balm of angelica

1. Pre-heat the oven to 400°F.
2. Beat the egg yolks with 2 tbsps sugar and lemon rind until thick and frothy. In another basin, whisk the egg whites stiffly with the remaining sugar, heap this on the yolk mixture and sift the flour on top. Fold all together thoroughly and spread on a baking sheet lined with nonstick baking parchment. Bake on the middle shelf for 8–10 minutes or until golden. Turn out the sheet of sponge onto a kitchen towel sprinkled with sugar, dampen the paper, and peel it off. Leave the sponge to cool.
3. Meanwhile, mix the lemon juice and water, take 5 tablespoons of it, and stir it into the cornstarch. Bring the rest of the liquid to the boil and pour in the cornstarch mixture, stirring constantly. Allow to come to the boil once, then remove from the heat and quickly beat in the

After the sheet of sponge has cooled, slice it into 4 equal strips.

Spread each strip with lemon cream and pile them on top of each other.

egg yolk. Whisk the egg white stiffly and gradually sprinkle with the sugar. Continue beating until the mixture is firm and shiny. Stir into the hot lemon cream. Sweeten to taste with sweetener.
4. Slice the sheet of sponge lengthwise into 4 equal strips. Spread the strips with lemon cream and pile them on top of one another. Spread all the sides with the cream, then leave in a cool place for a few hours.
5. Before serving, whip the cream stiffly, put into a piping bag, and decorate the cake with 10 rosettes. Stick a quarter of a lemon slice in each rosette with lemon balm leaves or angelica on either side. Cut into 10 slices. Refrigerate for at least 2 hours before serving.

Index